Photo: Oliver Wilson

Valerie Britton Wilson is a consultant specialising in social, political, organisational and marketing research, and a guest lecturer in qualitative research methodology. She has also worked in research and production for SBS and ABC television. Valerie holds an MA in political psychology from the University of Melbourne, and this book is based in part on her PhD from the University's Business School. Valerie is married with three children and lives in Melbourne.

the secret life of MONEY

exposing the private parts of personal money

VALERIE WILSON

ALLEN & UNWIN

First published in 1999 by
Allen & Unwin
9 Atchison Street, St Leonards 1590
Australia
Phone: (61 2) 8425 0100
Fax: (61 2) 9906 2218
E-mail: frontdesk@allen-unwin.com.au
Web: http//www.allen-unwin.com.au

National Library of Australia
Cataloguing-in-Publication entry:

Wilson, Valerie, 1947– .
The secret life of money: exposing the private parts of personal money.

Bibliography.
Includes index.
ISBN 1 86448 633 3.

1. Money—Psychological aspects. I. Title.

332.4019

Set in 11pt Weiss by J&M Typesetting Services
Design by Jo Waite Design
Printed by Griffin Press, Adelaide

10 9 8 7 6 5 4 3 2 1

Contents

Acknowledgements

Any project based on people-research depends on the goodwill and honesty of those who agree to be interviewed. I would like to thank all the people who so willingly shared their thoughts and experiences with me. In order to ensure their anonymity, identifying details have been changed and some of the stories that appear in these pages are composites of individuals or of incidents. If the stories, or the people, seem familiar it is because we can all recognise ourselves in the tales they tell.

Professor Amanda Sinclair, who supervised the PhD thesis upon which this book is partly based, was unstinting with friendship and guidance, inspiring greater effort at times when it was most needed. I thank her very sincerely. The Business School at the University of Melbourne provided a supportive working environment, and I am grateful to many people there. Through the University of Melbourne, I was granted financial assistance in the form of a Postgraduate Research Award and, later, a Writing-Up Award. The University's Statistical Consulting Centre helped with data entry and analysis of questionnaires. The ANZ Bank paid the out-of-pocket costs of running focus group discussions.

Dr Graham Little, Dr James Lees, Susan Lefroy and Professor Philip Williams generously shared the benefits of their academic and professional expertise in commenting on aspects of work-in-progress. Sue McFall contributed editorial assistance, intelligent comments on both manuscripts, and much-valued encouragement. Interest shown by friends and family — in particular, Kerstin McKay, Helen Saunders and Cara Britton — was always sustaining. I would also like to thank Vicki Tanner, Vicki Mimis, Peter Guy and Barry Fox, who have been particularly helpful at various stages of the project. Many other people have sent me books, articles or told me stories which they guessed, correctly, would assist in my quest to understand the private world of money. Still others — friends, acquaintances, colleagues and strangers — have contributed, sometimes inadvertently, to the money story in the course of casual conversations. I am very grateful to you all.

Jackie Yowell, publisher at Allen & Unwin, had faith that the thesis would be of interest to general readers, and encouraged me to rewrite it when this was the last thing I felt like doing. I thank her, and hope her faith will be rewarded. Editors Bryony Cosgrove and Christa Munns, as well as Jo Waite Design, brought their considerable skills to the final shaping and presentation of the book.

My husband John Wilson and children, Edward, Charlotte and Oliver, have put up with my preoccupation and made many perceptive comments along the way. From three-year doctoral program into book rewrite, the lengthy process would have felt impossible without their encouragement and forbearance. I thank them deeply for their support.

This book is dedicated to them, and to my parents, Pearl and Donald Britton.

Introduction

Is your own money harder to talk about than sex? Do you feel uncomfortable when your children ask you how much you earn?

There is more to money than meets the eye. Beneath its exterior life as a medium of exchange lies a complex and secret interior life. Money is not only legal tender it is also emotionally tender. Money officially inhabits a grown-up world but it speaks and acts with the voices of childhood.

Do you know how much your parents earn? Why does it feel so invasive if someone looks in your wallet? Do you hesitate to ask a friend how much they paid for that new couch or car? There is plenty of talk about money in the abstract — too much talk, some would say. But the inhibition about personal money-talk is puzzling, especially when the market view of money, as simply a medium of exchange, is so straightforward.

When I began to explore money as a subject for a research project, I was surprised by the responses it provoked among friends and colleagues. Some were very enthusiastic, sensing the possibility of buried treasure. Others were dismissive and made all sorts of suggestions about changing the subject: 'Why don't you look at income?' or 'Wealth — that'd be more interesting.' The word 'money' seemed to bother people. They would demand to know what I meant by the term 'money'. I thought I knew what it meant. I thought everyone knew what 'money' meant. An anthropologist has said: 'Everyone except an economist knows what money means.'[1]

These disparate reactions rendered the subject even more tantalising. What could lie behind this reluctance to accept 'money' as a topic for research? Why did people seem either appalled or enthralled? As it turned out, ambivalence and contradiction are characteristic of money attitudes: money is repellent yet riveting, private yet public, comforting yet discomforting. Money can be both too impersonal and yet too personal. Money attitudes are deeply linked to opposing psychological tendencies, the push and pull of which create an in-built tension.

When people say that 'money talks' they are usually referring to its bullying ability, its power to get what it wants, its power to control others. To say that 'money talks' may also be to acknowledge that money, like language, is embedded in our psyches. We take it for granted, and so its deeper role and meanings — as distinct from the mechanics of its more strictly economic role — are left unexamined. The language of everyday, personal money includes phrases that range from the sacred to the profane, from the 'almighty dollar' to 'filthy lucre'. But official money, the money of economics, keeps its language defiantly impersonal.

Linguistic contradictions underlie a deeper confusion. When you ask someone for their definition of money they will usually trot out a variation on 'it's a medium of exchange' or 'it's the stuff we use when we want to buy goods'. If this is all that money is, then why do people say they feel awkward, or embarrassed, when they have to talk to their bank manager or to their accountant at tax time?

Why is personal tax time so taxing? The tedium of collating data is real enough, as is tension about legal compliance, or making an error. But there is a sense of exposure when our personal money is laid out for scrutiny, and it is the rawness of this feeling that needs exploring. The feeling transcends income levels: it is not to do with amounts of money, or even the process of review, but with the unacknowledged complexities of personal money attitudes. We don't share our discomfort with others; it seems too shaming, too revealing, particularly when we like to think of ourselves, and to have others see us, as competent adults.

One of the things that attracted me to the subject of money was observing the difficulties parents have in deciding what to do about children and money. Do you see differences among your own children in their money behaviour? Is one a hoarder, another a spender? What do these differences mean? How much pocket money should you give them? Should they do tasks in exchange or should pocket money come as of right? Couples often disagree about the answer: differences in their upbringings and expectations are exposed in this mini micro-economic debate. In pocket-money discussions parents are conveying messages to each other as much as to their children. They inadvertently reveal a lot about their own attitudes to much bigger questions concerning life, values and expectations.

I looked to see what academic or marketing research had been conducted on attitudes to money but found it had largely escaped scrutiny. Considering that 'money makes the world go round', this gap in our knowledge seemed surprising. Even those organisations whose daily bread is money — financial institutions such as banks — don't really want to know about it. They may research attitudes to specific banking products, or banking services, but when it comes to understanding the raw material that underpins their stock-in-trade — people's attitudes to money itself — they turn their backs. Evasion runs deep. As a psychosocial researcher, with many years' experience in qualitative research, I grasped an opportunity to embark on a doctoral research program to explore the private world of personal money.[2]

It seemed to me from the outset that the subject 'money' needed to be left as open as possible, not crowded in by presuppositions. On the other hand, money is too big a subject to cover all its facets in one go. The task had to be kept within realistic limits. First, I decided to focus on the normal, everyday experience of money, as opposed to specific money issues or money disorders. Secondly, background reading and common sense suggested that factors such as gender, income level and cultural background may affect money attitudes. Since three-quarters of my own background is Anglo-Celtic I decided that this was the cultural group on which I would concentrate initially. People of Anglo-Celtic background remain the majority group in Australia's multicultural mix, and their values and perspectives still permeate our governmental and institutional cultures. It will be fascinating if future research can help us understand what elements of money attitudes are particular to certain cultures and what is universal.

The central part of the research was based on information from focus-group discussions, half with men, half with women. They included three different income levels: low, middle and upper. All participants were in the age range 35 to 55 years and had dependent children living at home. I chose this age range because these people were able to reflect on their childhoods as well as to discuss current money behaviour with their own children. I was also offered an opportunity to conduct workshops among some wealthy women in two Australian States. This was a valuable additional insight because money research has rarely included the perspective of the very wealthy.[3]

Overall, this is a view from households where someone is employed (or self-employed), representing about two-thirds of the Australian population in 1998. Nevertheless, many people in my lower- and middle-income discussions had experienced recent unemployment or were dependent on precarious employment. The money perspectives of those living in poverty or on welfare, and the effects of economic and social dislocation, have particularities that I have not yet covered.

This book is based on much more than the original formal research. Over the years that I have been exploring the subject of money the input has been voluble and voluminous, ranging across many different ethnic and socio-economic groups. Conversations at dinner parties or overheard in trams, radio and television programs, magazines and novels, have added to the information tapestry.

In the book the money story begins, not surprisingly, in childhood. People talk about their early money memories and trace the connections into adulthood. This may prompt your own memories as you read; it might even feel a bit uncomfortable. And there are some unexpected outcomes. For example, we like to think that what most affects money attitudes is how much of it we've got. A poor person, we assume, must feel very differently about money from a rich person. Income level, however, makes little difference to the underlying attitudes to money. The generous pauper and the wealthy miser are as widely found in life as they are in literature. Once we understand better the power of early childhood influences it is easier to see why subsequent income levels do not make the difference in attitudes we might expect.

What can economics tell us about definitions of money, and what can be learned from psychological and sociological research? We can see the contrast between economic, or supposedly *objective*, money and personal, or *subjective* money, between market currency and 'my' currency. We discover that money carries emotional baggage that severely hampers its operation as a neutral medium of exchange.

If money really were simply a medium of exchange, we

would not expect the mix of prudery and prurience with which people react to the subject. Exploration of this sometimes forbidden terrain exposes the 'underwear' of money. This is why reactions to the subject can be defensive, even hostile. British writer James Buchan describes money as 'frozen desire', capturing its transitoriness, its wishfulness and its passion.[4] Investigating the links between money and intimacy will help us to understand the emotion that surrounds money.

It is an important task precisely because money technology and currency are changing all the time. Childhood influences remain relevant no matter what physical form the official currency takes. As it is, our underlying attitudes to money have changed far less than the system that dispenses our money. This has practical implications for banking, for fund managers and fund-raisers, for governments trying to encourage savings, for mediators and counsellors — anyone who has dealings with people and their money. This book will start you thinking differently about money. It will show that our personal money attitudes, far from being rational and mature, are often irrational and infantile.

If money is the last remaining taboo subject, as some analysts suggest, then it is time we began peeling off the wrappings, so that we may understand better the power of this medium, both in our most personal exchanges and in those theories of economics that so dominate the world we live in.

Money Has a Childhood

If money is just a medium of exchange, why is it so complicated? A small business proprietor said to me that when he hears experts talking about money it sounds 'like other people's money'. One aspect of his response concerns language and the difficulty laypeople have with economic jargon. Another aspect, however, is that other people's money is a mystery to us because personal money is kept so secret. This leads us to imagine that other people are more competent at handling it than we are. Secrecy and wishfulness surround personal money.

If 'our' money doesn't feel like the experts' money, then what does it feel like? When we hear the word 'money', many of us immediately picture cash — notes, coins, dollars — or the dollar symbol. From a list they were given of eleven potential 'money' items, most of the people in my focus-group discussions selected banknotes first as most commonly associated in their minds with the word 'money'. Coins were next, followed by cheques. This indicates that, despite all the changes already upon us, and many more to come, the money of the mind is still tangible and traditional.

In his book *Minds, Markets and Money,* Israeli academic Schlomo Maital demonstrates the interconnection of personal psychological factors with national economic performance. He says that 'as individuals, we march along the milestones of our economic lives carrying mental baggage dating back to childhood'.[1] All of us carry this mental baggage, even if we are not aware of it. As with most baggage, it is made up of several layers. One of the first lies in childhood memory.

Memories and relationships

Most people I interviewed had clear memories of money in childhood, painting vivid, resonant pictures of their early lives: a physical landscape of corner milk bars, childhood bedrooms, money boxes, Sunday lunches, Christmas puddings and wide verandahs on sunny days. There was an important mental association between money and food, especially food treats such as ice-creams and sweets. Importantly, people mapped a detailed landscape of personal relationships that was quite moving. Their own attitudes to money, and memories of money, were often described in relation to the attitudes of important others in their lives: parents, partners, children. Immediate family members were the main characters in most stories, but grandparents or uncles and aunties who contributed special treats were sometimes fondly linked to early money memories. It is as if money cannot be talked about without connection to relationships. In this sense money is a deeply social substance.

A lower-income woman in her late thirties responded with this childhood story: **'My earliest memory is my grandmother's hand giving me those threepences. I just loved them. I thought threepences were better than sixpences because I liked the design better and I always associated that with buying an ice-cream, those threepenny cones. And I**

also remember vividly going with my mother to the bank, and going up the serious stone step. You felt really cheated when you gave them your full money box and all those pennies were just turned into numbers in a book.'

Contained here are several common themes in people's money memories: the inter-generational relationships; the enduring appeal of certain coins; and the association of money with food treats. In this particular story there is a warmth to the relationships; there is the sibilant description of entering a bank for the first time — that 'serious stone step' — and then the disappointment of gloriously rattling coins turned into a mere book entry. Three generations of family members make their appearance in that short response. Money has the capacity to provoke responses that uncover layers of family history — and family psychology.

An unhappy childhood?

Apart from the vividness of the physical and relationship landscape these money stories inhabit, another feature is the emotional landscape in which they are placed. In telling their money stories, people described sensations such as hunger, pain, satisfaction and pleasure, as well as emotions such as rivalry, tension, sadness, excitement and embarrassment. A high proportion of stories and memories were negative. Many people recalled their parents arguing over money; or they remembered the rising tension in the household when large bills came in; or they felt jealous of a sister who received more money than they did.

Money memories were amazingly fresh in the telling, containing long-lasting resentments, hurts, jealousies and some bitter lessons. The uncovering of family history and connections could be confronting. Descriptions were often emotionally charged and based on shame, guilt, denial, sibling rivalry, tension or sadness: **'There were five of us and Mum and Dad**

split up when I was quite young. Mum had to go to work. Money was always a pressure point in the family; it always seemed there was not enough and I guess I hated my mum having to go to work, she wasn't skilled.'

A schoolboy I talked to said his earliest memory was of his little brother almost choking to death on a coin in their Christmas pudding. When I asked how he felt at the time, he replied: '**Great — I hated him. Still do.**' His story revealed an underlying pathology that became increasingly apparent as our conversation progressed. It illustrates the power of money to expose the person, and the conflicts, within.

Asked for an early memory of money, people frequently confessed, for the first time, to stealing from a parent's wallet. In the words of an upper-income woman in her mid-forties: '**The first thing I thought about was when I stole money from my mother's purse. What I remember was the lack of reaction from her. It obviously wounded her to the very bone, and I wasn't punished, but I knew what I'd done. It was never raised again, ever, but oh boy it's left a memory!**' The sense of guilt associated with this act of domestic treachery remains vivid and unresolved, despite the passage of years.

On the surface, some stories are simply about money and making ends meet: '**We always had a boarder, an old lady who lived in the front room. When I was about thirteen, I remember Mum saying, "All the fruit that you get — you wouldn't have it if Miss Watkins wasn't living here." I remember telling this to a girlfriend. One day, we had a fight and she threw it back at me, "Oh, you wouldn't have any fruit if you didn't have Miss Watkins in your house!" I also recall that when I was about fifteen, Mum used to go somewhere during the day. When I'd get home from school she wasn't there and I never knew where she was, because our family didn't sit round the table and talk. She must have been ashamed or something but I eventually worked out she was cleaning houses to get a little bit more money.**' This story is rich with information about social position, about the importance to a family of keeping up appearances, about their eating habits, their communication patterns, and about the perils of friendship.

Men and women volunteered different kinds of money memories. Most men recounted pleasurable early money memories, associated with food and motherhood or money gifts from indulgent relatives. Women were more likely to describe early money memories that were so entwined with stories of family relationships that it was as if the one (money) could barely be discussed without the other (family).

This tendency for women to connect money to key relationships, as well as a tendency to recall negative emotion in making that connection, are both vital pieces of information. Women are often less accustomed than men to dealing with money, and research, as well as anecdotal evidence, shows that women are less comfortable with money than men. The proliferation of 'Women and Money' courses, designed to help deal with this discomfort, provides further evidence. My research indicates that women may transfer negative childhood associations, consciously or unconsciously, onto money in adulthood, which complicates their response. Money, for women, is entangled in a web of relationships and negative emotions. If this tendency could be understood, then more could be done to help women (and many men as well) to disentangle some of the emotional complexity that may be inhibiting their ability to deal rationally with money.

As part of my research I asked people to note the emotion they most associated with the word 'money'. The results showed that money is associated as much with pain as with pleasure. The main emotions people volunteered were, in order of frequency:

- worry/anxiety/concern/depression/stress/panic
- pleasure/happiness/enjoyment
- desire/greed/need

- satisfaction
- freedom
- security

In an American survey by Carin Rubenstein, involving 20 000 respondents, anxiety, depression, anger and helplessness topped the list of selections from a range of adjectives provided. Happiness and excitement came next, followed by envy, resentment, fear, guilt, panic, distrust and sadness. In the choice of negative emotions, women consistently outranked men.[2] I also used a scaling technique to delve further into some of these associated emotional meanings, and this again showed women to be more negative about money than men. Although women would appear to have a particular difficulty with money, neither men nor women immediately think positive thoughts when they think about money.

Nothing in my research findings suggests that money can buy happiness. Worries and unhappiness predominated. Happiness was not a word people used much in connection with money, except to question the connection. When I asked 'What is the most important thing your money gives you?' people said 'independence', 'choices', 'freedom'. The words 'pleasure' or 'fun' made only fleeting appearances in money-talk and reminiscences. In fact, money seems to be an overwhelmingly serious thing for most people.

If happiness is an absence of worries, then money can buy some of that. It can buy freedom from worry about essentials such as food, shelter and health care. Studies indicate, however, that if we are freed from those worries we turn our minds to other worries of a more self-reflective nature, to do with personal and interpersonal problems. Ironically, these are areas where money has less power to relieve the worries.[3] Research shows that happiness and life satisfaction are different, and that neither is highly correlated with income level. An increase in income and material wellbeing does not necessarily increase our general sense of wellbeing. Anyway, we tend to judge ourselves not by 'objective' measures, such as median national incomes, but in relation to those around us. We make these subjective comparisons covertly because money is one of the great secrets of life, beginning in childhood.

Hush money: secrecy begins in childhood

For many people, the childhood atmosphere surrounding money was characterised by silence. Money was not a topic discussed in front of children. Details of earnings, or of financial arrangements, or money problems, were kept secret. Some children were told specifically that money was not to be discussed. Parents said it was 'bad manners' to talk about money, often adding that money-talk was 'vulgar'.

For others, the secrecy wasn't explicit, but '**you just understood**'. The atmosphere conveyed was all the more powerful for being largely tacit. One wealthy woman said: '**It was awesome in its secrecy. The only clues you got were papers on the desk and hushed conversations that you might half overhear.**' A middle-aged man in a lower-income group said: '**My parents were pretty secretive about what they earned. They never talked about it with each other or with us kids. Even now I have no idea how much money they have.**'

Parents today like to think they are more open about discussing money with their children. In practice, however, there is still a high level of secrecy. More than three-quarters of my adult respondents said they did not know their parents' income. When asked if their own children now knew their parents' incomes, almost the same proportion said they did not. So the change from one generation to the next is minimal, income level remaining a highly guarded secret. Some people bristle at the thought of their money world being questioned by their children, or by anyone else. One man said: '**I hate my children asking me how much we earn. I really object to that. To me it's almost like an invasion.**'

Australian sociologist Supriya Singh commented: 'Money is so private, that persons do not discuss the issue of privacy.' None of her Anglo-Celtic sample had discussed their financial affairs with their children and very few said they would talk about money with their parents. She says: 'It is as if the privacy of money draws a circle around the couple — excluding children, parents, siblings and friends. This is true for those in their 70s and in their 30s. It is one of the characteristics of marriage money that has not undergone a generational change.' In Rubenstein's survey, quoted earlier, a similar pattern of reticence was discovered: two-thirds of the parents in the sample hadn't revealed their income to their children and almost half would rarely or never discuss money with their parents.[4]

When asked why they avoid being open about money with their children, people usually justify it in terms of 'protection' rather than secrecy: **'I try to keep a bit of shelter there. My daughter once asked if we could have a swimming pool, and I said we couldn't afford it. A few weeks later she wanted to know if we could afford a packet of chips! So it concerned me that she had started to think we couldn't afford to live. It's too complicated.'**

Parents like to say that children need protection from 'hassles' or 'worries' associated with money, and that they won't understand the complexities of value-differences associated with money. They are ostensibly protecting their children from these complexities, but they are also protecting themselves from the difficulties of teasing out their own money attitudes, at risk of revealing the extent of their own immaturity and irrationality about money. Nevertheless, the desire to protect children from money worries is real enough. In families where financial circumstances improved during a person's childhood, money was more likely to be talked about than in families where financial circumstances remained constant. Where financial circumstances worsened, the silence increased.

There are plenty of rational and practical explanations for

keeping facts about personal money from children, but this chronic secrecy about money needs further examination. Rational explanations don't account for the extreme discomfort, the coyness, the evasion that parents often exhibit when their children, or others, attempt to get close to their personal money. This awkwardness is transmitted across generations. 'Why,' asked a friend of mine, 'did neither of my children, when applying for their first casual jobs, ask how much they would be paid?' Knowing her well, I suggested that she herself would have avoided asking such a question, and that even though she may never have said anything explicitly about not talking about money, they had picked up her reticence, the sense that it is a forbidden topic.

Why does it feel so invasive to be asked questions about your own money, especially by your children? Another rational explanation for reticence is to say that children do not understand relative value — to them $1000 is a fortune, therefore a salary figure will sound huge even if it is minimal. We worry that it may lead to unrealistic expectations or constant material demands. We worry about the use of the information, imagining salary figures being bandied around the playground at school: 'My dad earns more than yours.' Kids 'showing off' may distort the truth. Use of the information may be inaccurate, it may be flattering, but it may also be humiliating. It is out of our control. The following two stories told by fathers, both lower-income, illustrate the problems of inaccuracy and loss of control:

'My son said he tells the kids at school that we're poor because "You keep saying we can't afford to go on this excursion". I got angry and said, "Don't you ever say that we're poor. We're not poor, we're probably in the top 10 per cent of the world. We're well-off compared with 90 per cent of the world." I really wanted him to get the perspective on that because he'd got it out of perspective.'

'My son goes to school and tells everyone we're rich! I

say, "What do you mean we're rich? We're average mate, average, which means we're not poor and we're not rich, we're average. We'll have people knocking on the door!"'

In discussing their children, adults reveal their own anxieties about the 'relative' nature of money and its capacity to provoke envious comparison. Both the men quoted responded to their children with a disproportionate pugnacity. In using taboo words such as 'rich' or 'poor' their children inadvertently, as well as inaccurately perhaps, reveal parental secrets and threaten the Australian desire to be seen as average. These sort of reactions illustrate a tendency for men to perceive money as an element of competitiveness and power, or powerlessness. There is anxiety about being laid bare, about the relative status money may reveal, and an uncertainty about how to deal with children and this issue. Deferral and hedging, therefore, become features of inter-generational money interactions.

Another reason for the reticence is that money is, or can be, used for social comparison and judgement: the view that people are what they earn. People may look down on me if I earn less. Or people will expect certain things of me, or certain attitudes from me, if I am perceived as wealthy. People will judge me successful or unsuccessful by the amount I earn. And how will they judge my spending priorities? We may like to deny it, but we do tend to be judgemental about other people and their money.

Money as a medium of morality

Money is cloaked not only in mystery but also in moralism. This is evident both in child–adult and in adult–adult relations. Children were, and still are, taught 'Save before you spend'; part of an educative process, ostensibly about money, but with larger ramifications. Parents like to tie money to 'moral' lessons involving denial, restraint and delayed gratification. Adults often comment upon other adults' financial arrangements in a self-righteous tone (especially when they disagree or disapprove). Judgements about others are made on various financial levels, ranging from pocket money for children to large purchases, trips, loans, credit-card usage and general spending patterns.

The air of moral righteousness is also apparent in the paternalism of banks, an attitude that leads people to feel, resentfully, that they must justify their spending. A 1993 study in Britain explored attitudes to debt. Despite clear-cut evidence that the cause of indebtedness was mostly external (that is poverty), those interviewed tended to say others were in debt due to greed and lack of self-control, observations that are moralistic, judgemental and intolerant. A British study of pocket money noted a similar tendency for advice given to parents on this subject to be moralistic.[5]

It is common for something that has psychological value to also be ascribed 'moral' value. For parents, educating children about money raises it above the crudity of material exchange to a more elevated dimension. When personal money does emerge from hiding it often encounters this moralistic environment, the metaphorically pursed lips of disapproval. There is disapproval, for example, of 'easy' money. It should be hard-earned and, when it is not, it must be shady, illicit, loose, immoral. People look favourably on royalties earned from an invention, less favourably on rental income derived from property. There is also disapproval of people who simply 'do' money differently. The self-righteousness of the financially careful can sound particularly pious. British writer Jan Pahl notes in her book *Money and Marriage* the 'astonishment' expressed about other people's financial arrangements. There was not only a difficulty in understanding differing arrangements, but an unwillingness to do so.[6]

American economist J.K. Galbraith commented that 'much discussion of money involves a heavy overlay of priestly incantation ... Those who talk of money and teach about it and make a living by it gain prestige, esteem and pecuniary return, as does a doctor or a witch doctor, from cultivating the belief that they are in privileged association with the occult ...'[7]

The secrecy surrounding personal money, together with the sometimes impenetrable jargon associated with official money, means that communication between the two worlds is extremely difficult. Add to that a sense of overbearing moralism, and it is no wonder that people keep their private money world to themselves.

Learning that money is serious

When telling stories recalled from childhood, people described a sense of great seriousness about money, sometimes approaching reverence — one simply didn't joke about money: **'From a pretty early age we were conscious there was some kind of big deal about this issue. It was something you took very, very seriously. Huge! You didn't mess about with money.'**

This seriousness often became apparent when children lost money, even small amounts. There were stories of siblings dropping a coin on the way back from shopping for parents, and the enormous fuss this would cause. At the time, it had seemed out of all proportion and felt vaguely unjust. These adults, however, talking in the 1990s, had parents or grand-parents who had experienced, directly or indirectly, the Depression and world wars, upheavals which understandably affected money attitudes. Much of the caution, the negativity, the seriousness, can be attributed to an underlying fear of serious economic and social dislocation that is difficult for younger generations to comprehend. A lower-income woman in her mid-thirties recalled: **'One thing I remember from childhood is really hating my parents' attitude to domestic life. No leftover food was ever put in the rubbish bin, it all** went into the fridge, suspender clips were cut off, everything was kept. As a kid I remember hating it. It was because they were both teenagers during the Depression. I could understand it but I loathed it. And now I'm doing the same thing! It's got nothing to do with unemployment.'

Adults today talk to their children about money in much the same way as their own parents did. It is remarkable how little the specific admonitions have changed: we tell our children to save, to spend wisely, to avoid credit and to work hard. In many cases this represented a conscious and deliberate effort on the part of parents to pass on what they now regard as sound advice, as the following comment from a middle-income man illustrates: 'We learned that we never got anything for nothing. We never got handed pocket money, we had to earn our pocket money. And my boys are the same. They've got to do a job. You don't get anything for nothing, it's not a free ride. I instil that into my boys now because I have a work ethic. I don't mind working, which my father instilled into me. He said: "If you're a hard worker and your bosses can see you're a hard worker, then you'll always have a job." And that was driven home.'

A few other people I talked to expressed some doubt about the appropriateness of this almost reflex advice in changing times. Another middle-income man observed: 'We were a single-income family with five kids so there wasn't an awful lot floating around spare, and that was just a fact of life. Dad was a teacher so he had a regular income, and it never really changed that much. We were never poor or broke but we never seemed to be flush with funds either. The subject was never really discussed. I can remember as a little boy having a bank account and pocket money weekly; I think the idea was you learned how to manage your money. The same thing I'm doing with my daughter now basically. I often wonder why, because back then you were building up credits with the bank or institution for a potential housing loan in twenty years' time. But nowadays you can just do it over the counter in fifteen minutes and it just doesn't seem to matter. There doesn't seem much point in developing the concept of savings for the kids.'

Only a minority of the people in my research were reacting against their own childhood experiences or parental advice. The following two quotes were both from lower-income men, suggesting that abandonment of the traditional parental prescriptions may possibly lead to less successful financial outcomes:

'My mother and stepfather didn't talk about money a lot; they used to fight about everything. My mum used to encourage me to save, to sort of be careful with money. With my kids I'm a bit of a softie. I basically try and give them what they want ... we're not rich but I never worry about money. I talk about money pretty openly with people.'

'I don't think I ever went without and I think I got all the platitudes like "Look after the pennies and the pounds will look after themselves". I don't think it ever did any good. There was just this disconnectedness. Little pieces of information would come to me but it was a thing that wasn't talked about. My mum and dad both worked really hard for the family's money. But I looked at what they were giving me as pocket money and I thought, Well that's never going to amount to much, I mean at 25 cents a week I am not going to have a million dollars by the time I'm thirteen. And so it always seemed an impossible task — you know, "How do you eat an elephant? One mouthful at a time." Well, if I'd learned the lesson about one mouthful at a time I probably would've saved. But I didn't. I used to get this 25 cents, look at this "elephant", which was what I was saving up for, and say "Look it's just not going to happen". And go and buy some lollies!'

Most of today's parents continue to pass on to their own children a lot of the caution, fear and negativity that their own parents had conveyed about money. Above all, today's parents still lament the lack of seriousness with which their offspring regard money: money left lying around, small coins not picked up. Their children are not according money its due seriousness. They are underestimating its value; not so much its literal value as its symbolic value. Parents wonder: Is this indicative of a potential flaw in my child's financial character?; Don't they realise how hard I work to earn money?; Why don't they see that every little bit adds up? These may be perennial intergenerational refrains, the older generation always seeing the younger as excessively offhand, verging on profligate, in their money attitudes and behaviour.

Or parents certainly fear that this is so. Much of the money-talk that passes from parent to child is based on undiagnosed, perhaps even unwarranted, fear. This is the basis for the specific maxims and admonitions about money that do break through the silence, attempting to underscore its seriousness.

Money maxims

The big childhood money message for the adults that I interviewed was about saving: '**It's always been drummed into me to save; I'm sure I was born with it. Whatever you earn, put something away.**' For some, a nexus was established in their childhoods between a work ethic, earning, saving and responsibility. This seemed particularly true of people who are now in higher-income brackets, though their parents were not necessarily well-off. These may be adult justifications for current attitudes, rather than something genuinely learned from parents. It does seem to have had a successful financial outcome, however, since they are now better off than their parents and on higher-than-average incomes. Higher-income people, particularly men, told stories of explicit educational elements in their money childhoods: '**It was an impression about the value of money: don't throw it away, save it for that rainy day;**

make sure you spend it wisely; earn it before you spend it and so on. I guess the time my father did teach me something was when I was buying a car. My parents could have lent me the cash but they didn't. They took me out to a finance company where I got a loan for $1000 to add to the $1000 I'd saved, and I bought an old Valiant. I paid it off after two years. I think they gave me the money to pay it off anyway, but it was all a lesson about finance.'

Apart from saving it, the other important lesson conveyed in the childhoods of these adults was that money is hard-earned, so spend it wisely. An atmosphere of seriousness surrounded money — it should not be parted with lightly: 'I can remember vividly I badly wanted a bike with gears, so I found one and negotiated the price of $25. I went to ask Dad for some money and he said "no". But there was 100 feet of agricultural drain he wanted dug down by the back of the house and we agreed I would dig that. It took me three weeks and I got $20. He was happy to give the money but never an advance; I had to earn it first. This impressed on me that it didn't represent a piece of paper, it actually represented three weeks' work!'

Listening to people talk about money, one would suppose Australia to be a nation of serious savers. Not everyone accepted this childhood lesson, however; some had rebelled against it, hating the pennypinching carefulness of their parents. Some described irritation felt for mothers who would go home for a cup of coffee rather than pay to have one at a cafe. The saving of those pink, cut-off suspender clips, mentioned earlier, is particularly poignant. This sort of scrupulous saving felt irksome rather than admirable (even when we later find ourselves doing the same).

Many factors have subverted the strong saving message of childhood: including economic pressures, consumerism, advertising pressure and credit cards. Research in the United Kingdom has shown that optimism or pessimism about the future is an important factor in saving rates.[8] People think that if the future is predictable and likely to be better, then it is worth saving for. If not, then live now, spend what you've got and let the future take care of itself. If governments are serious about wanting to raise the level of personal savings, they should take heed of such money experiences and attitudes and use the knowledge and insights as a basis for campaigns to reinstate the saving habit. Most adults in Australia today had saving messages drummed into them by their parents, and these messages are lying not far from the surface. Despite all the changes, today's parents are still saying much the same things to their own children, even though they sometimes recognise the illogicality of such reflex responses: **'There was definitely an atmosphere of encouragement to be thrifty, to save, to not spend beyond your means. I suppose I try to pass that on to our kids, a saving ethic. But you wonder, when today's society seems geared around just go and get a loan, spend it now, and don't worry about later. Maybe that's not a bad philosophy. I'm not sure, I'm thinking about it! It's interesting — our childhood gets locked in the back of the brain somewhere, and it's really difficult to change even though society changes around us.'**

Money memories matter

Are past experiences and memories relevant? The doubters are quick to point out that the technology of money has already changed enormously. Cash as we know it will soon be nothing more than a quaint relic, joining cattle, beads and shells as items of anthropological interest. Thus the memories and maxims we have uncovered could be irrelevant. And although current emotions are real enough, the specific memories described by people may not even be accurate: they are the adult memory of childhood, with all sorts of denials and glosses in place.

This doesn't detract, however, from their power, or from their continuing impact. For all their inaccuracies and subjectivities, these memories remain relevant and important because they have not gone away. The stories people told were particularly evocative: of time, of place, of era and, crucially, evocative of important relationships. In addition, the stories are important because they are so emotive. The emotion sometimes could be pleasurable, but was more often unhappy. Either way, negative or positive, the memories are personal and often delicate. In addition, they are usually hidden, not talked about, even to oneself. They can therefore be a powerful source of often unconscious emotion and tension. This has important implications for anyone dealing with people and their money, in banks or other financial institutions, who may trample, albeit unwittingly, on sensitive, unacknowledged personal memories.

People also carry specific baggage in the form of parental advice and maxims about money. These admonitions represent more than just a set of instructions. They incorporate a parental value system that, whether followed or not, lurks not far from the surface in adult psyches. Either in emulation or rejection, current adult money behaviour and attitudes are rooted in these maxims. Precisely because change is so rapid, people cling to old verities as an anchor of certainty amid all the change.

In his paper 'The uses of childhood', political psychologist Graham Little describes 'the ways childhood can be used in the service of both identity and ideology, the personal and political uses of childhood. This is childhood as a construct, selective, open to revision, shaped by what we are about, and a childhood that is carried about in grown-up heads belonging not to the past but to the present, a part of who we are now.'[9] In this way, money memories remain relevant to the present. As Little says, childhood may be 'out of sight but not out of mind'. Memories of money continue to shape contemporary adult experience.

While these early childhood memories are important, they are just the tip of the emotional iceberg. Beneath the conscious memories is another level that seems to vindicate or at least illustrate psychoanalytic ideas about money. As we listen to money speaking, to the personal voice of money, the underlying issues become clearer. Our money attitudes, secretive and unthought-out, are forced into the open when we have to confront the normal run of external economic necessities and pressures. Material demands made by children can function as a sort of crucible. We then experience money as more than a medium of material exchange: it becomes a medium of complex psychosocial exchange.

Touchstones: Money Coming Out

As we have seen, most people are raised in an atmosphere in which money, explicitly or implicitly, is a taboo topic. Money-talk within the family is circumscribed, and ignorance about financial affairs across generations within a family is widespread. Personal money attitudes are kept hidden, and it usually takes some external pressure to force them into the open. Children are often the source of such pressures within the family, and one of the regular themes that emerges in intergenerational money relationships is the deferral of gratification: Why do we tell children, 'We can't afford it', even when we can?

Deferring pleasure: money doesn't grow on trees

Today's parents tell their children three main things about money: save it; spend it wisely; realise that it's hard-earned. These maxims have changed little, if at all, from those handed down by earlier generations. Writing about the nineteenth-century rich, British economist John Maynard Keynes commented: 'The duty of "saving" became nine-tenths of virtue … Individuals would be exhorted not so much to abstain as to defer, and to cultivate the pleasures of security and anticipation.'[1]

To underscore and implement the three maxims, parents invoke another three — deferral, denial, and doubt. These are expressed in the common refrains: 'Maybe next week' (defer, delay); 'We can't afford it' (deny); and 'Do you really need it?' (doubt).

The use of timing/delay as a way of conveying the value of money was, and continues to be, a feature of parent–child money relations. In response to a request for a particular item (often clothing or toys), parents will say something like 'We can't afford it now, but maybe next week'. This is meant to indicate that money has first to be earned before it can be spent; that decisions have to be considered; that spending ought not be impulsive. With any luck, the desire itself may fade in time. This tactic lends a sort of gravitas to material exchange while giving parents a decision-making breathing space, a chance to 'buy time'. It offers a counter to what many see as the excessive ease of modern money, combined with constant pressures to consume. It acts as a pause on the spending button and is part of educating children away from the notion that money comes easily. Whether there is money to pay for the requested item is irrelevant; discipline and self-control are being taught. To defer pleasure — 'Maybe not this week' — rather than to deny it, seems an appropriate way to show the link between spending and saving or to negotiate the balance. The capacity to defer gratification may become an end in itself, an opportunity to pass on something of more enduring value to one's children. Here are comments from four mothers in one of the upper-income discussion groups:

'I think children take it for granted that everything's handed to them, and I just don't believe in that. Sometimes it would have been easier to hand them the money but I say,

"We can't afford it".'

'I disagree with that. My children don't ask for outrageous things, and if we can afford them, why not? We could get hit by a bus tomorrow!'

'I don't always say "yes", but I do sometimes feel that way afterwards. Why say "no" when we can afford it? I think it's better for them, though, if they realise they can't have everything straight away.'

'I feel like that, too. It's nice to give them things and let them do things and enjoy their life, but I think they have to know that in life things aren't like that; you can't always get what you want.'

At a less conscious level, parents are struggling with their own uncertainty about the appropriate balance between spending and saving, and perhaps some unease about their own tendency towards more immediate gratification. 'We can't afford it' is a response most commonly heard in middle- and upper-income families. It is symbolic rather than factual; parents are more likely to say 'We can't afford it' to their children when they can afford it. It is an exercise in control of gratification, a part of the lesson 'money doesn't grow on trees'; first it has to be earned, then saved, then spent wisely. Parents fear that their children won't appreciate what they've got, that they may 'expect it all on a plate'. Attaching qualifiers such as 'We can't afford it at the moment' or 'I'll think about it' represent a use of parental control while sounding reasonable and open to persuasion. It is also a symptom of the uncertain ground in changing values and demands across generations.

Use of the phrase 'We can't afford it', particularly in relation to children, was one of the few areas in my research where people's income level did make a difference. Middle- and upper-income people frequently employ the phrase as a constraint on materialism and complacency. By contrast, people on lower incomes try very hard *not* to say 'We can't afford it', even when they can't. Their prime concern is to avoid infecting their children with money worries, to cover up, to protect. To say 'We can't afford it' seems too discouraging, too worrying, a reminder of financial constraint: **'I hate my husband saying to the kids "We can't afford it". I don't think he should say it; they're sick of it. I try not to say that.'**

There are times, even for the wealthy, when things genuinely can't be afforded, either at that moment in time, or ever. And there are times when people *feel* as if they can't afford things, even when they have the money. 'We can't afford it' is a very controlling phrase, a hard-to-argue-against retort. To take a stand against it risks seeming irresponsible or profligate. Because risks and consequences are so easily imagined and because information about money-matters is still enveloped in privacy, the person using the phrase usually gets their way.

American psychiatrist Edmund Bergler set out a simple dichotomy about this: '*Normally*, the phrase "I cannot afford it" is a simple statement of objective fact. *Neurotically*, the phrase "I cannot afford it" represents a defensive triumph against psychic masochism.'[2] In subsequent chapters we will hear more about this psychic masochism. Bergler was describing those who deny themselves, rather than deny others, though they probably do both. My research has demonstrated, however, that the phrase is often *not* a simple statement of objective fact. Nor can its use always be taken to represent severe neurosis. It shows that there is important territory to explore and understand around normal, everyday money attitudes, which is not necessarily psychopathological and which has often escaped attention.

Another common tactic in the normal round of money-games is the strategic injection of doubt. To be asked 'Do you really need it?' can feel worse than the more categorical 'We can't afford it'. 'Do you really need it?' appears to put the onus on the would-be spender at the same time as it effectively undermines them. It plants a vigorous seed of doubt, ready to sprout into all its unspoken corollaries, like: It doesn't suit me anyway; I've already got lots of pairs in the cupboard; Can I really afford it?; Am I just being greedy?.

'My parents used to say "We can't afford it" and "Do you really need it?". Then they had my younger brother, ten years after me, and I felt that he was brought up differently from us because by then finances were a lot easier. He wasn't brought up with that "No, we can't afford it". But with my children, even if we can afford it I still say "No, we can't afford it" because I want them to see the importance of saving. It's not a lot of money they're getting, probably 20 cents or something, but to me that's a grounding in what happens if you save, that small money mounts up to big money. And that's really how we were taught, too.'

Here are echoes of sibling rivalry, the effects of changing financial circumstances, and yet the pervasive strength of financial admonitions across generations. It shows that we do carry the baggage of childhood into our adult relationships with money and into dealings with our children.

Deferring payments: attitudes to credit

Closely linked to the general belief that deferring gratification is good for you are the attitudes to borrowing, debt and credit. The belief in savings, combined with suspicion of credit, were common themes in the childhoods of all income groups in my research. Credit carried a stigma for the older generation. Purchases made on credit were a sign of desperation and/or flawed character: 'Nothing's for nothing, you have to earn it'; 'Pay cash'; and 'Provide for your children'. These were the refrains of childhood, often accompanied by tales of those who had failed to heed such lessons. There was also a pervasive emphasis on ownership of the family home and thus on paying off the mortgage before anything else:

'My mother said never lend to anybody. The first thing a bad bloke will do is bite you for a bit of money and never, never agree. Marry a man with a good job. Dad's attitude was "An honest man never made a million". You shouldn't just throw it away; it was really important to have something there to provide for your children, and you should never put children under threat. He'd say, "It's really easy to lose it". There was this notion of going too far, and for him you never borrowed money to buy something for yourself. You might borrow to buy something for your business if you thought it was wise, but you were a real idiot to borrow money for a car.'

'My dad always used to want us to pay cash for everything. He'd say, "If you don't have the cash, don't buy". It's as simple as that. Even as a teenager, discovering layby, my dad didn't even like that. We'd say to him, "But Dad, you don't have it until you've paid for it". To him, though, unless you handed money over and received something, everything else was a form of credit.'

Attitudes to credit have changed enormously, though there are some adults who still cling to the belief that credit is inherently bad. Though debt and credit are not quite the evil of the past, this attitude still retains a certain fervour. There is a feeling that credit can do harm, that it is safer to stay with what you have, what you can control. This attitude, though probably more common in lower-income groups, can transcend income levels, as revealed by two upper-income men:

'I bought my first car on hire purchase. It was a conscious decision at the time: "Yes, I can pay it off." But I think with a family, four children at a private school and not wanting to be hit at the wrong time with an interest slug, I just tend to steer away from credit altogether. I just don't use credit.'

'I try to avoid credit too. That's perhaps something my parents have passed down.'

The majority of adults these days, however, recognise the value of using credit. It is part of a 'living life now' philosophy and a reaction against their parents' tendency to postpone pleasure. Many of today's parents believe that their own parents were over-careful in husbanding their financial resources as insurance against possible misfortune. They feel saddened and even irritated by their parents' inability to let go financially: **'They've got the money, but they can't spend it. I see that they are in a trap really. I'm not the same as they are. I think if you've got the money you should enjoy it, not leave it till you're too old or sick.'**

For women this took a more circumspect form, likely to translate financially as 'Spend what you have rather than put it off'. For men it was more likely to mean turning to credit as a means of obtaining more, sooner. Men were more comfortable than women with credit:

'I watched my parents develop their quality of life, and it was a painfully slow process. The temptation is to use credit instead of paying for the extension on the house. I think everything's a lot faster, and you need the money to come faster to keep up, to acquire what you want.'

'I see credit as a tool. You might want a big holiday in October that's going to cost twelve grand. I've only got eight disposable so do I sell some shares or do I just use the Visa card? And it probably just goes through on the Visa card, knowing I'll catch up in two months' time. Rather than worrying about dropping off something that's important to you, you use credit as a short-term tool. I wouldn't borrow money to have a holiday and pay it off over five years, that's not what it's all about, but for short-term purposes we do that. I don't think I'd borrow 40 grand for a new Mercedes or something. That's not the way I'd play it.'

There is a mismatch between rhetoric and practice. The current generation of children is growing up with parents saying one thing and doing another. They still impress on their children the importance of saving, and they employ all the standard refrains to deny or defer gratification. Parents sometimes recognise that their behaviour belies their words, in contrast with that of their parents, whose messages and actions were more likely to be consistent. There is also another kind of denial going on: the fact that people don't see credit as debt. They espouse inherited anti-debt, pro-saving ideals while at the same time run up bills on their credit cards.

An inter-generational tussle may be perennial, even inevitable — the older generation bemoans the lack of seriousness with which the young treat money, each generation using money as just one way of differentiating itself from its parents. It remains fascinating to see just how potent the earlier parental discourse about money can be. There is a sense of parent admonition hovering over the adult shoulder even as behaviour changes. A form of behavioural rebellion is taking place while still reciting the stern parental money maxims. This adds to a sense of discomfort about money: people struggle to move away from the constraints of their own childhood, with varying degrees of awareness of the hypocrisy of the position they adopt in relation to their own children. Their saving message to their children has a different emphasis, being less attached to moral virtue or an end in itself. The purpose of saving is spending — to buy something better. It is saving to consume: **'We try to teach them to respect money. It's not the be-all and end-all, but if you're going to work hard for it, don't just throw it away. Enjoy it, but if you accumulate that little bit you can buy something nicer.'**

Pocket money: a bob each way

It is often easier to expose underlying money attitudes by talking to people about specific instances of money in action. Pocket money and restaurant tipping, for example, bring money attitudes into the open in a way that reveals differing priorities. Pocket money was one of the issues that prompted me to research the subject of money. Two aspects were interesting. One was the way in which parents seem to get tangled up in something as apparently simple as pocket money: When should children start getting it? How much? How often? What, if anything, should be expected in return? The second was that these decisions unveiled a range of underlying differences that were not only about pocket money.

Parents taking part in my research discussions adopted different methods of paying pocket money to their children. These ranged from payment of a small amount of cash each week to cash payments made fortnightly or monthly. Some operated a 'book' at home through which pocket money was administered, while a few paid a sum directly into a child's bankbook each week, in one case as a direct debit from salary. Mothers were usually the primary dispensers of pocket money, especially for younger children. Once banks or larger amounts were involved, or children were older, fathers sometimes took responsibility. Amounts varied from 10 cents a week to 20 dollars a week, depending on the age of the child and the expectations involved. Income level did not much affect the amounts; other issues were at stake.

Three main streams of underlying behaviour tend to be encouraged or expected by parents. There are those who pay pocket money as of right and expect nothing specific in return. There are those who expect certain specified household chores to be completed as a pre-condition for receipt of pocket money. And there are those who give money as of right but at the same time stress the general obligation to contribute to household chores. Importantly, for this group, actual performance of chores is deliberately not linked to payment of pocket money.

Adelaide researcher N.T. Feather found that the two main purposes for giving pocket money were 'independence-training' and 'meeting children's needs'.[3] Underlying these were two basic value orientations: one towards strong belief in the work ethic and individualism, the other emphasising social welfare values, family and communalism. Individualist values emphasised the need to earn the pocket money while pro-social values resulted in pocket money being paid as of right. Mothers were more likely to emphasise the communal, the maintenance of family harmony, while fathers were more likely to stress the individual.

We saw earlier that the more 'educative', exchange functions of money had been impressed (or so it was perceived, with hindsight) upon those individuals who were now in upper-income groups. It is not possible to know whether this is an accurate rendering of past parental practice or justification of current practice. It would seem to indicate, however, that the 'earn-it', individualist approach in childhood is more likely to lead to some economic success. Either way, it is invoked by a higher-income group experiencing economic success in their own right. Perhaps, therefore, the 'as of righters', the communalists, may be paying a future price for their children's economic lives in exchange for family harmony bought with childhood pocket-money practices. Feather suggested that future research should look at ways in which parents might find a balance between protecting family harmony while still promoting their children's individual development.

By learning something about market exchange, about 'give and take', about negotiation, the 'earn it' pocket-money group is trying to modify childish egocentrism, to help children understand that money is not 'on demand'. Nothing is for nothing. Conversely, there is a fear in those who believe in 'as of right' pocket money that these market processes and values will enter the domestic world, that children might expect to negotiate a price for every task and every contribution to family life. In trying to decide on a pocket-money option, parents may see, sometimes for the first time, that they don't agree with their partner, or that each has brought different mental money baggage into the relationship. Even if there are no differences between them, the pocket-money option that parents adopt (and the rationale behind it) may then be exposed to the scrutiny not only of their own children but also of other adults and children. We have already seen that people are often judgemental about the money paths others take if it is different from their own.

The parents in my research gave pocket money in order that their children might learn to save, learn to spend and, for the 'earn it' group, learn to earn. It was thought that handling pocket money would teach children to manage amounts over time, to plan, to budget, 'to experience the responsibility of money'. They would learn about making decisions, making mistakes, and about banking skills. Almost as a postscript to these educative functions was the hope that children might experience the pleasure of money.

In practice, parents displayed varying levels of attempts to exert control: some children were free to spend the money as they wished; others were required to save a portion; some had to come to their parents for the money; others had it credited to bank accounts. Belief in the necessity to 'learn to save before you spend' was widespread. It was applied almost instinctively, in the absence of advice or knowledge to the contrary. It is based on a fear that children may tend to the spending equivalent of jumping in the deep end, a fear exacerbated by the ease of obtaining modern money. Some research evidence lends support to the importance of learning to save. One study measured children's knowledge of money and their experience of money. Children who had saved up for something had higher knowledge scores and higher experience scores. By contrast, earning the money did not affect the scores as much. Having money to spend was also of value in gaining knowledge, and both saving and spending were more important, in this respect, than the earning of money.[4]

A British survey looked at age, gender and class differences in pocket-money practices, and noted that the tendency to ew she had to make arrangements for the baby to be after. She rang several nanny agencies and, when I o her, their brochures had arrived in the mail. 'I can't nyself to open them,' she said. 'It seems too crass, w, this exchange of money for my baby's care.' In this the money may have been a symptom of a more sig- reluctance to leave a child in care, or to return to work, imes like that money can seem particularly cold and priate.

izer suggests that domestic monies, such as holiday Christmas money and so on, are 'socially constructed ies, shaped by the domestic sphere in which they cir- and are vastly different from the 'instrumental, ratio- model of market money'. She says: 'Contrary to the equation of money with power and rationality, amounts ne do not in themselves determine their uses or control; cation of household money always depends on com- btle understandings about relations among household rs.'[7]

ket money is an example of the subtlety and com- of money within the domestic sphere. But it is more is. In his book *The Money Motive*, Thomas Wiseman has out that money in childhood is part of a complicated control, often dressed up as education.[8] He reminds us ldren have 'reversal fantasies', in which they dream of the tables on the father, of having more than the father, controlling him in turn. This Oedipal response is seen dly in stories of the mega-wealthy: the Packer and h families come to mind in Australia. Recurrent media tion about arrangements for transition of money and o the next generation in these families may reflect an fascination with familial rivalries. In the Murdoch case, de even more interesting by the rivalry between a male emale heir-apparent. Several of the wealthy women in arch were engaged in a complex battle either to outdo

save, or not, was pretty much fixed by the age of eight.[5] The authors of this survey noted another study that discovered pocket money was sometimes given for the purpose of taking it away. Use of pocket money for punishment (by confiscation) is a very explicit exercising of money, power and control. Although an extreme example, it illustrates the capacity of something as apparently innocent as pocket money to open up not just psychological, but even psychopathological, under-pinnings. Money can be used as an instrument of cruelty, an aspect that emerged in some of the stories of wealthy people discussed later in this book.

The educative role of pocket money was illustrated in a story told by wealthy American philanthropist Tracy Gary at a Westpac Private Bank seminar in Melbourne. She recalled her first pocket money: '**My parents said I would get 50 cents a week. They laid out five separate dimes and said, "Here is your pocket money. You could spend one, you could save one, invest one, give one away, you might even lose one." This made me see the different functions money could play.**'

Tracy Gary has gone on to a lifetime of work advising other wealthy women, investing in ethical projects and sup-porting charities and educational programs.

Her story encapsulates American social anthropologist Viviana Zelizer's view that money, far from being standard and homogeneous, is multiple and complex. It is subject to a variety of forms of 'earmarking' for varying purposes, full of symbolic and personalised meaning. Zelizer describes 'special monies' and 'culturally invented' boundaries for money. For example, she says: 'the resistance to pay children for house-work, as the reluctance to compensate housewives for their work, points to the use of money as a boundary. If domestic tasks are paid "real" money, then the family becomes another commercial setting.' And again: 'Normative expectations of the family as a special noncommercial sphere made any overt form of market intrusion in domestic affairs not only distasteful but a direct threat to family solidarity.'[6] This, as I saw in my own research, is the position of the pocket money 'as of righters', the communalists.

With the increasing length of time that children are engaged in tertiary studies now, the issue of allowances for older student-children raises the same questions as did earlier pocket-money decisions: How much? What, if anything, in return? In Australia, payment options for university fees (Higher Education Contribution Scheme or HECS) have exposed another aspect of money attitudes. Differences between individuals, and between families, become evident as decisions have to be made about whether to pay the university fees upfront or defer and default to the income-tax system. Some parents, if they can afford to, like to pay upfront and avoid having their child incur debt. Others believe strongly that it's up to the child to make their own way and pay off the HECS debt when they can. Still others tie their contribution to the child's results.

The dilemma is about dependence versus independence, control versus letting go, about when and how and at what price the cord should be cut. Perhaps we remember stories about Rupert Murdoch being taught to swim by being tossed in at the deep end by his father, or Kerry Packer being sent straight back by train to his boarding school in another State to pick up a tennis racquet he had left behind. Is this, or the equivalent, what we need to do to make our children successful? In a small way, pocket money is an early indication of our attitudes.

Beyond pocket money and allowances, an increasing number of young adult children in employment choose to continue living at home. This then raises the question of 'reverse pocket money'. How much money, if any, should children who are earning independent incomes while still living at home contribute to the household expenses? Does it feel bad to take money from your children? 'Not at all,' say some parents. 'It's

their fathers or to 'pay them back' by 'doing money' differently. American psychoanalyst Sheila Klebanow says: 'An individual may strive to earn a great deal of money or very little money or something in between for many reasons. Identification or disidentification with one's parents, competitive strivings with the oedipal rival, its absence, or its intensity are of paramount importance.'[9]

In the various parent–child money scenarios we have explored, people rather zealously defend whichever option they have adopted. Because we are often dismissive of other people's money choices, when the tables are turned, their scrutiny — with its imagined, implied, or even explicit, criticism — feels unpleasant. So it reinforces our desire to keep money private. When people are asked whether they would talk about their personal money habits outside the family, they will usually respond: 'It depends.'

Money-talk outside the family: the importance of equivalence

People told me they may discuss money with close friends, but most still see money as a private subject. This was true of all the income groups with which I spoke:

'No, I wouldn't choose to talk about it to people unless I was very close to them. I think it's not something I feel comfortable discussing with people.'

'I agree I don't like talking about how much money I've got — it's sort of a private thing.'

'I would never say what we earn or what we bring home.'

'It'd have to be an appropriate time. I mean, I wouldn't mouth off at a morning coffee with girls I play tennis with, but if it was an appropriate time and an appropriate response I wouldn't care. They can know how old I am and what religion I am.'

People often find money easier to discuss with strangers, and they seemed quite comfortable with the subject when they took part in my research interviews. Similarly, professional money relationships, as in talking to a financial adviser, are predicated on detachment. When people took part in my discussion sessions they were recruited into groups of similar income level. This was important because it was clear from my findings that approximate income parity is a prerequisite for talking about money with others. Some of the wealthy women I interviewed had previously attended a 'women of wealth' workshop. They described the catharsis of declaiming, publicly, 'I am wealthy', for the first time in their lives. They had even been encouraged to write the precise amount of their wealth on a piece of paper. One recalled: 'We screwed up the paper and dropped it on the ground behind us.' Self-exposure was possible only among income equals.

There is often a sense of shocked outrage if someone schooled in money-silence, inherited from childhood, meets someone not similarly schooled. As with nudity, money revelation can involve an uncomfortable sense of exposure, even indecency, particularly if it is one-sided. This sensation can be experienced by the person forced reluctantly to reveal something of their personal money life, as when someone asks what you've paid for something, or when you are forced to discuss your income or savings with an outsider. Equally awkward is being on the receiving end of a private money revelation from someone who is not similarly inhibited; not only is it unwanted but it feels somehow wanton.

People of all income levels usually resist discussing publicly the precise details of their incomes or of their spending. Most people said money-talk was acceptable in certain situations, but only if it remained general. To discuss actual amounts was described as 'crossing the line' or 'a bit tacky'. Rough income equivalence — real or perceived — enables greater openness, as this exchange in a middle-income group indicates:

'I can talk to my girlfriends who are in the same field as I am. I can say, "How much are you getting an hour?"'

'But would you ask someone who was getting double your salary how much they get?'

'No, I certainly wouldn't. If I wasn't sure what figure they'd be on, or if I knew they were quite wealthy I probably wouldn't want to ask.'

'It's on a similar scale to asking someone what their bank balance is. I mean it isn't something you have a right to know, even if you want to know. It's their personal, private affair.'

People think that if they reveal their incomes, or spending details, they may lay themselves open to criticism and judgement. And given the moralising that goes on around money, this is a realistic apprehension. The following two comments, the first from a low-income woman, the second from a middle-income man, illustrate the hesitance:

'For me it depends on who I'm talking to whether I feel free to talk about money or not. If I'm talking to somebody who I know is in a similar situation, we can have a good whinge about it! We know each other's financial situation and it's similar. But if it's somebody who perhaps has quite a bit more then I tend to feel a little bit shy about the fact that we're struggling.'

'In general terms, yeah, not a problem. But I think if it was too specific you'd leave yourself open to criticism. I think different people have their own ideas about managing things. Some people never borrow money and I know people who borrow regularly, for their own reasons. But it doesn't matter what you say, you'd leave yourself open to criticism.'

When asked to consider these questions, people are often bemused by their own inhibition. One woman said that before she came to the discussion her mother and father had dropped in to show off their new car. She wanted to know how much they had paid for it but couldn't bring herself to ask. Why did she imagine it might be 'offensive' to ask this question? We apply for jobs and don't ask about the salary. Do we imagine the prospective employer may think less of us? That we are only doing it for the money? It does seem extraordinary that we display such hesitance. The sociological explanation concerns money's position as a unit of social comparison, of relative status or success (even though people may feel that money ought not to exercise this function). To reveal one's personal income or details of one's spending priorities, whatever one's income, is to risk revealing too much about oneself:

'The measure of your worth tends to be how much you earn. So if you earn 25 grand a year and you sit next to somebody who earns 50 grand, somehow or other you feel inadequate.'

'It's not because it's money, it's because it's more personal. I think how much you earn is a status thing.'

'It would be very easy to offend other people by talking about your own situation, so it's safer to stay away from the topic.'

This sort of reaction was particularly common in the middle-income groups. One obvious explanation lies in this need for income parity as a precursor to any sharing of personal income information. At middle-income levels, income boundaries are less precise, more fluid, and that sense of parity can be more elusive.

Do men and women differ?

Women were more likely than men to talk about money with close friends, usually other women. It was described as 'chit-chat' about money, rather than significant discussion. Most, though not all, felt comfortable talking to their husbands about money, and it was seen as indicative of a good relationship to be able to discuss and deal with money issues together. Even within marriage, a *sense* of parity is an important precursor to communication. In Meredith Edwards' Australian study of financial arrangements in families, she noted that the more wives earned the more likely were husband and wife to communicate about money and also to jointly control and manage it.[10] Women set more store by openness than the men in my research, and were more likely to maintain that they talk to their own children about money than were the men. As Carin Rubenstein's survey discovered, however, secrecy increases with income level, and men were the primary income earners in my study.[11] Also, women tended to think that money is less tied to status and power than do men:

'I like talking to women about how to save it, how to get something for less, and I can talk about that endlessly!'

'I talk very freely here, it doesn't bother me. But probably in front of men who are using money as an ego thing I'll say nothing because I just don't want to get into their game.'

'It wouldn't be something that I would talk about at a dinner table with partners, but I might bring it up in conversation with a girlfriend.'

Some men said they would discuss money with 'close mates', but only if they thought their income levels were roughly similar. Their money-talk concerned getting advice from others about tax or investments, for example, or discussing a particular purchase item — generalities rather than personal details:

'It's not something that's done in my circle of friends, outside of a one-on-one situation. In my circle there are a lot of self-employed people and I guess you're either doing well or you're not doing so well. I guess we talk in generalities not specifics.'

'I'd rather talk about cars or sex or football or something!'

Income categorisation provides an interesting insight into males and money competitiveness. The people who took part in my group discussions were recruited according to income categories using census data as guidelines. In addition, I asked participants to note the income group to which they felt they belonged — upper, middle or lower. This self-definition exposed some fascinating gender differences. Using the objective census income guidelines, I had recruited one-third of respondents from each income level. In the subjective rating, however, only 5 per cent of men placed themselves in the lower-income category, compared with 30 per cent of women. Lower-income men were more likely to score themselves upwards, as middle-income. Both men and women preferred to avoid describing themselves as upper-income, in this case both choosing the middle-income label.

Important gender differences were described in the previous chapter on childhood memories of money. There was shared territory for both men and women in the physical landscape of early money memories, and there were similar memories of parental maxims and admonitions. Women, however, were more likely to carry the money-discourse further into personal relationships. For women, money-talk seemed inextricably linked to the emotional landscape of relationships, current or past.

By contrast, men were more likely to discuss money objectively and to look outwards from the personal into the larger economic landscape of Australia and overseas. Men were also more likely to perceive a competitive element of money (and it may have been this very competitiveness that led them in the research groups to try to sound knowledgeable about larger contexts). Unlike other research projects where men are frequently more difficult to 'draw out', this did not hold true for money discussions. The talk, however, did tend to take this different tack. It required constant effort to keep men's money-talk personal (where it felt a bit uncomfortable) and resist their attempts to depersonalise by talking about banks, economic conditions or other areas where they felt more comfortable.

What the experts say: my money versus their money

How do people reconcile, if at all, their own private money worlds with what they read or hear about money from other sources? The external world of money-talk, the terrain of economists and other finance media experts, inevitably impinges on the private money world. People do listen to what such experts say. Some take it in as part of the general political landscape; what is happening on the economic stage is seen as directly and indirectly tied to the political world. Some listen for specific purposes — notably interest rates — that affect their personal financial affairs. Currency news is followed closely by those engaged in businesses that may be affected by exchange rates.

There was some evidence in my discussion groups, however, that women feel more detached from this type of money-talk than do men. For some women there is 'my money', which is personal and understandable, and there is 'everybody's money', which is impersonal and difficult to grasp:

'I listen to it with a sort of mild general interest. There's not much one can do about it all. It doesn't sound like my money. I feel rather removed from it; I don't feel it's my money they're talking about.'

'It's not so personal; it's like group money, everybody's money.'

'I do listen to a certain point but I don't get worried or upset if they're forecasting doom and gloom. Maybe that's a safety thing for me; it's other people, not me, it doesn't directly affect me. Maybe I'm in a fool's paradise.'

'When they talk about the Budget being blown out by this much, I've had men say to me, "You just don't understand because you're female". But I think whoever's got to budget — whether I've got a budget for home or whether Joe Bloggs has got a budget for the whole country — a budget's a budget. And then I think of my father, who said, "If you

haven't got it you don't spend it". I can't see why the same principles can't apply for a 100-dollar budget as for a 100-billion-dollar budget.'

In the last comment, childhood money memories remain pertinent to the adult's world view. The father's admonition was located firmly in the centre of the child's domestic money world a generation later. That viewpoint was then transferred to the broader economic and political stage. To some economists it may seem hopelessly simplistic, but it is clear that early money memories and maxims are carried into adulthood. Rightly or wrongly, people will judge politicians and economists on the basis of such conflations.

Official money, or expert money, and its language, provides sharp contrasts with the personal territory we have been exploring, and the following chapter takes a detour into this world.

3

Expert-talk: Money in Economics

We may not take money, the substance, for granted, but we do tend to take money, the word, for granted. When I was asked by people, usually men, what I meant by 'money' I realised I would have to arm myself with some knowledge. With no training in economics, I assumed I could turn to that discipline for an answer. I assumed there would *be* an answer. Surely economists know what money is. I was to discover that debate about what constitutes 'money' was more complex than I had imagined.

Money, in the form of coin, is thought to have been 'born' in a temple. The word is from the Latin *moneta*, the name of the goddess in whose temple money was said to have been first minted — ironical in the light of subsequent biblical references to moneychangers and temples. I looked in dictionaries for standard definitions and found money, as we know it, originally defined as 'metal stamped in pieces'. Today, it is assumed to be composed of metal or paper (though we need to add polymers to the list). Since Aristotle's time, money's functions have usually been described as: 'a medium of exchange'; 'a measure of value'; and 'a store of value'. Two later additions were: 'a unit of account' and 'a measure of deferred payment'.

The allure of cash

Economic anthropologist Walter Neale makes useful distinctions between money as 'stuff' (an actual physical item), money as 'idea' (for example, when we compare the value of two things), and money as 'process' (promises fulfilled or debts paid). Neale clearly explains the standard list of money functions:

> As a *medium*, money is a way-station in the exchange of goods or services sold or rendered for goods or services purchased. This function has been expressed in the formulation 'Goods into Money into Goods', meaning that in this function money is but an intermediate, convenient stage in converting one kind of good into another. In the sale the money is equated with the good or service sold; in the purchase the money is equated with the good or service purchased. It has thus served as a *standard of value* for each good (or service) sold and purchased. In the time between sale and purchase the medium thus served automatically as a *store of value*. Since the medium thus already serves as a standard of value and a store of value, it is an obvious choice to express promises to pay in the future in the same units, thus making money a standard of *deferred payment*. When a notation is made about money as a standard of value or as a standard of deferred payment, or when any other record is made of a money valuation or transaction, money is often called a *unit of account*.[1]

Money as physical stuff is powerful stuff. Historically, people have fiercely resisted any changes to the stuff of money. Paper money, which we now take for granted, came to be deemed money, first in the form of promissory documents, and later as banknotes. This did not happen without a fight from bullionists who defended money of intrinsic metal value against the incursions of something as ephemeral as paper.[2] Any modification of currency — from gold to silver, then to copper or nickel, then to paper, and then to other forms of banking money — always resulted in warnings about real and tangible value being undermined. In London in 1857, Lord Overstone fulminated against the suggested inclusion of bank deposits as 'money', declaiming: 'Precious Metals alone are money. Paper notes are money because they are representations of Metallic Money. Unless so, they are false and spurious pretenders.'[3]

People and nations become attached to existing forms of currency. There was uproar in England when it came off the gold standard after World War I, and the very expression 'floating the dollar' gives the sense of a currency breaking its moorings. In 1998, as the European Economic Community (EEC) has fought to introduce a common currency, and as the cashless society approaches, the strength of attachment to existing forms of money is again exposed. The childhood history underpinning an individual's identification with his or her own particular currency is a potent factor in this, and one that has not been acknowledged. People fear that change will undermine 'their' money, and, since money and the person are so linked, change can feel like a personal affront.

Money is often defined by what are regarded as its essential characteristics: portability, divisibility, homogeneity and acceptability. Money must be practical. We need to be able to carry it around; to divide it easily into smaller or interchangeable amounts; and it needs to be standard, consistent, homogeneous. Of the four essential characteristics, however, the most interesting is the notion of acceptability. It is the social conventions that underpin acceptance of certain substances as the unit of exchange that give money its power.

Anthropology is especially enlightening about the role of social acceptability. Anthropologists writing about exchanges in primitive economies, such as the use of cattle or shells, have helped us to understand the cultural and social conventions on which money is based. We forget that today we are doing the same thing when we accept certain coins and notes, or cash substitutes. We, too, are deferring to custom. The nineteenth-century economist Carl Menger said: 'Thus money presents itself to us, in its special locally and temporally different forms, not as the result of an agreement, legislative compulsion, or mere chance, but as the natural product of differences in the economic situation of different peoples at the same time, or of the same people in different periods of their history.'[4]

Definitions, analogies and language

As I investigated the definitions of money it became apparent that not only the money itself but also the definitions have evolved as money's functions have evolved. In the seventeenth century, for example, a new element was added to the standard list of money's functions as a by-product of expanding exploration and international trade. British philosopher John Locke acknowledged that money was derived from 'common consent', with its value not just fixed and unchanging but having a 'facilitating' function.[5] This more fluid conception of money's function was tempered by his concern about deterioration of the coin itself, revealing a continuing belief in intrinsic bullion value. Similarly, trade expansion and exploration led British political philosopher Thomas Hobbes, in the mid-seventeenth century, to his description of money as the nourishing lifeblood of the State:

> By Concoction, I understand the reducing of all commodities, which are not presently consumed, but reserved for Nourishment in time to come, to some thing of equall value, and withall so portable, as not to hinder the motion of men from place to place; to the end a man may have in what place soever, such Nourishment as the place

> affordeth. And this is nothing else but Gold, and Silver, and Mony ... By the means of which measures, all commodities, Moveable, and Immoveable, are made to accompany a man, to all places of his resort, within and without the place of his ordinary residence; and the same passeth from Man to Man, within the Common-wealth; and goes round about, Nourishing (as it passeth) every part thereof; In so much as this Concoction, is as it were the Sanguinification of the Common-wealth: For naturall Bloud is in like manner made of the fruits of the Earth; and circulating, nourisheth by the way, every Member of the Body of Man.[6]

Most descriptions of money in economics texts employ scientific language and, in particular, the language of physics and mathematics. Hobbes' description of money as the lifeblood of a nation was unusually human. Much later, the nineteenth-century British economist Alfred Marshall argued that biological analogies were the most appropriate for complex economies and should supplant the mechanical analogies of earlier economics:

> Consider, for instance, the balancing of demand and supply. The words 'balance' and 'equilibrium' belong originally to the older science, physics; whence they have been taken over by biology. In the earlier stages of economics, we think of demand and supply as crude forces pressing against one another, and tending towards a mechanical equilibrium; but in the later stages, the balance or equilibrium is conceived not as between crude mechanical forces, but as between the organic forces of life and decay.[7]

Karl Marx was also an exception, employing language that was thoroughly visceral in attacking the evils of money capitalism.[8] He described the greedy capitalist as having a 'werewolf-like hunger', a 'vampire thirst for the living blood of labour', and money as the element estranging man from man and man from himself: 'money is the *pimp* between need and object, between life and man's means of life'. Marx saw money as the ultimate alienator, 'an abstraction from its *specific* personal nature'. Though his is a fundamentally different conception of money's function, the language is reminiscent of Thomas Hobbes' blood metaphor from two centuries earlier.

Perhaps it is unfortunate that, as Israeli academic Schlomo Maital points out, Alfred Marshall's argument for more human principles in conceptualising economics was eclipsed in favour of the mathematical abstractions of another economist, Leon Walras: 'Walras's analog was the planets. The mathematical tools that show how the stars and planets impinge upon one another cannot, by themselves, reveal how human beings impinge upon one another.'[9] This illustrates the way in which a discipline can be hijacked by its ruling metaphors, and the importance of language in defining response. Official money-talk is all about velocity, balance, equilibrium, currency, resources, deposits — a lexicon associated with measurability and order. The language is neutral, kept well away from the messiness, disorder and emotion of real people's relationships with money. If economics had retained biological metaphors, perhaps people would feel less alienated from its dicta. Or perhaps hiding behind scientific abstractions has been deliberate, a convenient mystification, keeping the 'expert' safe from the layperson. The mechanical language of economics keeps money removed from human biology, from Alfred Marshall's 'organic forces of life and decay'. When money is so central to daily life, this official language defines priorities, and those priorities at present keep people out. Modern economics keeps money bloodless.

In my search through economics texts for the nature of money, I had not expected to find warmth and humanness but I had expected to find precision. I had thought that by the twentieth century economics would be able to supply a clear answer to the question, What is money? At first glance it seemed straightforward. The composition, functions and essential characteristics of whatever a society deems 'money' can be specified, and indeed they are in 'standard' definitions. Disagreements about what constitutes money, however, have continued from Aristotle to the present day. Current debates make matters even more confusing. In seeking precision, paradoxically, money has become even more elusive.

Today we have terms such as 'commodity' or 'definitive' money — based on coins having intrinsic value — versus 'representative' or 'fiat' money of no intrinsic value, such as notes. That seems a simple enough distinction. The question remains, however, as to what precisely should be included in even this definition of money. J.M. Keynes used the phrase 'current money' to mean currency (coin and paper) plus bank deposits, including unused overdraft facilities. There is also the notion of 'transactions money' which includes cash plus 'chequable deposits available on demand'.[10] Under this definition, term deposits would not be deemed 'money'. This becomes a question of 'velocity' — if money is not 'on hand' is it simply deferred, or temporarily out of circulation? The crux is accessibility and the essence of the definition becomes 'liquidity' — the more the funds are liquid, the more they are 'money'.

Money turns out to be a question of degree and timing after all. The discovery was rather unexpected, but I took comfort from the fact that noted economic historian J.A. Schumpeter agreed: 'there is no denying that views on money are as difficult to describe as are shifting clouds.'[11] By adopting the language of the physical sciences, and by its use of mathematical models and charts, perhaps economics has created a rod for its own back. We expect answers and solutions and we expect them to be correct. When they are not forthcoming, or when they are wrong, we become cynical, or perhaps relieved and even pleased, and relish anti-economist jokes, like 'Economists have successfully predicted nine of the last two recessions'.

Is money neutral? This is another area where the interconnection between language, expectations and disciplinary boundaries can be seen. For economists, the question of neutrality refers not to matters of intrinsic worth, nor to absence of emotion, but rather to function. Does money in itself have an inherent effect on prices, on inflation, on the economic process? Or is its intrinsic effect nil? Is money an empty vessel, merely functioning as the passive medium of exchange of standard definitions? Political psychologist Robert Lane points out in *The Market Experience* that the concept of neutrality flows hand-in-hand with a belief in rationality: rational individuals and a rational market.[12] He demonstrates that such a narrow reading of market economics is inadequate in the face of evidence from psychology, anthropology and sociology. The themes already explored in this book — the childhood of money, the privacy, the complexity — undermine any argument for rationality.

In 1776, Scottish political economist Adam Smith argued that a bank should not advance more than the amount of capital a merchant would normally have kept by him in cash.[13] This conjures up a vivid mental picture of sacks of cash, or the piles of coins pictured in childhood pirate stories. Smith's caveat may be increasingly pertinent today. The financial excesses of the 1980s were often ascribed to entrepreneurs who had lost a sense of money-reality, for whom money had no tangible anchor. Similarly, the use of plastic money or digital money may detach us as individuals from a sense of ownership. This is why casinos issue plastic tokens in place of real cash. 'Our' money, real and tangible, becomes play money, fun and eminently loseable. Australian social researcher Hugh Mackay commented that 'managing money is actually harder than it used to be. When money is invisible and intangible, the very concept of money changes and, except for the more sophisticated users of the system who rapidly adapt to it, the sense of control over money recedes.'[14]

Changes to money have made it simpler to transact, but in other ways money has become both more complex and more subtle. Yet, when you say the word 'money' people still picture cash. In 1859, Karl Marx said: 'the primitive economic superstitions of people and governments cling to tangible, palpable and visible bags of money.' Research data from my study, and from a much larger European study, confirm the importance to most people of real money, rather than abstractions.[15] Marx had the right word: this attachment is *primitive*, and therefore ought not to be underestimated. When the basic urges that underlie our attitudes to money are taken into consideration, then it is easy to see why, for example, the European Economic Community has taken such a long time to negotiate agreement on a united currency, the Euro. Primitive urges are ill-understood, poorly articulated and often repressed. And we tend to underestimate their power to prevail over reason.

Philosopher Georg Simmel described money as 'interchangeability personified' and, in this sense, neutral — a symbol of relativity. Yet money is anything but neutral and is deeply 'personified', though not in the sense Simmel had in mind. For most of us money is still something tangible, palpable. Money is also the stuff of dreams, hopes and fears. It is used to convey messages to children about value and values, to teach partners a lesson when they are unfaithful, to control, to cajole, to manipulate. Money speaks, but in many tongues. There is much more to money than meets the economist's eye.

What Can the Social Sciences Tell Us About Money?

The silence about money in the personal domain is equally apparent in the academic domain. Researchers Kent Yamauchi and Donald Templer said in the 1980s:

> Although money is an important feature of modern living, there is a dearth of empirical material and only a limited amount of relevant theoretical and clinical information on money in the psychological literature. It has been noted that more information on sexual behavior exists than on money behavior.[1]

Most of those who have approached the subject comment on the scarcity of research and information. British researcher Adrian Furnham suggests three possible explanations for this gap in our knowledge: 'a lack of rapprochement between psychology and economics; a lack of standardised instruments for assessment; and a taboo associated with money.'[2]

Psychological approaches to money

What research there is reveals money in a markedly different light from that shed by economics texts. In the psychological literature, the impersonal or depersonalised meanings of money are replaced with a sense of money pregnant with personal meaning and far from neutral. Political psychologist Robert Lane comments: 'Income and money, with their implications for rank, deference, prestige, and all the trappings of wealth and power, imply two of the most affect-laden elements of life. The negative emotions may be even stronger: fear of failure, of unemployment, of bankruptcy, of humiliation.' And again: 'money is symbolised in such a way as to be phenomenologically anything but neutral; it is invested with a variety of fears, obsessions and inhibitions that distort its serviceability for market calculations.'[3]

My research was an attempt to find out what, if anything, might lie beneath espoused money-talk. I thought it was possible that attitudes to the substance 'money' may have changed far less than the systems that dispense money. Do phrases such as 'the rattle of coins' or 'the rustle of crisp banknotes' still create resonances for people? Does greater ease of money access and exchange create new anxieties? Does the use of cards as substitutes for 'real' money push money 'underground' and exacerbate a sense of facility outstripping reality? Psychology is one discipline to which we can turn for some answers.

Since the 1980s, interest in money as a subject for research has grown. Most tends to focus on particular aspects of money such as gender differences, inheritance, children and money, money and motivation, compulsive disorders (such as overspending, gambling) and psychotherapy and fee-paying. My interest was in exploring the money of normal, everyday experience, and here the data sources were more limited.[4] There are, however, some studies where the notion 'money' is confronted head-on. They have attempted to pinpoint money by devising scales that could first define, and then measure, the meanings people ascribe to it.

One study explored the meanings of money in order to

gauge its value as a motivator in an occupational/organisational context.[5] It was found that various occupational groups responded differently to money as a motivator. For example, hospital sisters were less likely to be motivated by money than sales people, technical people or managers. The study concluded that generalisations about the meaning, role, or value to the individual of money cannot be made. This is useful but not surprising as we all know that some of us are more motivated by money than others (though employment practices do not always acknowledge this difference).

More interesting was that, of the seven main meanings of money that emerged from this research, the top-ranked cluster was described as 'shameful failure'. The primary meaning of money for many people was found to be as a potential source of degradation and embarrassment, of worry and anxiety; an orientation that was independent of actual income. Money seen as benign, good and socially desirable came only second in the rankings, and the practical value of money (comfort and security) came fifth out of the seven.

Similar negativity about money was uncovered in an American study involving 20 000 readers of *Psychology Today* magazine.[6] While the sample was perhaps atypical, and certainly self-selecting, again there was a predominance of negative emotion connecting to money. From a list of twenty words representing emotions associated with money, the four most likely to emerge were 'anxiety', 'depression', 'anger' and 'helplessness'. Women nominated all four more frequently than did men.

The survey also found widespread secretiveness about money, over half agreeing with the statement that 'it is generally prudent to conceal one's income from family and friends'. Men were more secretive than women and secretiveness increased with income level. The author suggested a pattern of inter-generational taboos surrounding money: over half of this adult sample had not revealed their income to their parents, while almost two-thirds had not revealed their income to their own children.

There was more evidence of inherited attitudes in the study's so-called Midas scale: 'spenders' versus 'self-deniers'. Those who described themselves as free-spenders or extravagant were more likely to be healthy and happy. By contrast the deniers had lower self-esteem, were unhappier, more pessimistic about the future and had more psychosomatic problems. Most said they had parents who were the same.

British researcher Adrian Furnham explored the connection between personality traits and money attitudes. His results suggested a 'complex web of associations' with some connection to demographic variables such as age or gender, and some connection to psychometric variables such as anomie, protestant work ethic, conservatism and so on.[7]

In the United States Yamauchi and Templer had looked at the work of psychotherapists and personality theorists such as Freud, Klein, Adler, Fenichel, Fromm and others.[8] Based on this theoretical background, they defined three broad areas of the psychological aspects of money:

- Security, including optimism, comfort, confidence, and their opposites, pessimism, insecurity, dissatisfaction.
- Retention, including parsimony, hoarding and other obsessive personality traits.
- Power/prestige, incorporating ideas of status, importance, superiority and acquisition.

The researchers then developed a set of 62 statements exemplifying each of these three aspects, such as: 'I put money aside on a regular basis for the future' (security); 'I hesitate to spend money, even on necessities' (retention); 'I use money to influence other people to do things for me' (power/prestige). After a sample of people rated these statements, five key factors emerged:

- Power/prestige: the use of money to impress and influence others and as a symbol of success. High scorers indicated the importance of status-seeking, competition, external recognition and acquisition. Low scorers minimised the importance of money to achieve these.

- Time-retention: high scorers placed great value on preparation and planning, with future security as the goal. Low scorers were more present-oriented.
- Distrust: high scorers were hesitant, suspicious, doubtful, whereas low scorers seemed trusting and accepting in money situations.
- Quality: high scorers were those who believed in getting the best and/or paying the most to get the desired quality. Low scorers placed little purchase emphasis on quality.
- Anxiety: high scorers on this item saw money as a source of anxiety as well as a source of protection from anxiety. Low scorers conversely were less anxious about money situations, less worrisome.

From this, the authors developed a Money Attitude Scale that they tested alongside standard psychometric measures of paranoia and anxiety. Two aspects of their findings were of particular interest to me. The first was that scores on the five main factors of money attitudes listed above were independent of actual income. The second was that, comparing their original list of hypothesised content areas with those that arose from what people said, two additional factors had joined the list of key variables and both were negative: distrust and anxiety.

Another researcher, Thomas Li-Ping Tang, developed a Money Ethic Scale, which he tested in the United States and Taiwan.[9] His work also interlocked money attitudes with broader life/work orientations and he claims that 'people's attitudes towards money, as measured by MES [Money Ethic Scale], can be perceived as their "frame of reference" in which they examine their everyday life'.

These various research studies revealed emotional aspects of money that were frequently negative. In some cases it may have been self-fulfilling, the researchers' own unacknowledged negative predispositions about money (worry, awkwardness, guilt) permeating the studies. The *Psychology Today* study, for example, asked people which feelings they could recall associating with money in the past year. The list given to respondents included fifteen negative adjectives but only five that were positive. In that study, as with others, 'retention' is assumed to be negative and self-deniers are then found to be unhappy. In Yamauchi and Templer's study, the statement 'I am bothered when I have to pass up a sale' is included as an indicator of anxiety. This presupposes negative meaning and doesn't recognise that there are those for whom bargain-hunting may be pleasure or sport.

Most of the cognitive factors uncovered in these studies are concerned with aspects of power (of relative status, social comparison, respect, control) and of freedom (freedom, too, can be an aspect of power). Material comfort and security receive less emphasis, perhaps assumed, or subsumed, within notions of power and freedom. The behavioural factors (budgeting and so on), the domain in which 'official' objective views of money might be expected to hold sway, seem almost a postscript, an incidental aspect of money-meanings when explored from a psychological perspective.

Overall, the studies reveal several important factors about money attitudes: negativity is prevalent, perhaps even predominant; attitudes are often independent of income level; attitudes are complex and multi-dimensional; and money attitudes may provide a sort of individual psychic barometer.

It is curious, however, that for all the rigorous testing, the careful design and analysis in these studies, one is left feeling no closer to understanding people's real attitudes to money. The 'factors' identified fail to capture the richness of meaning, much less the nuance and the paradox. Widespread negativity is uncovered and identified but not explained. It is ironic that attempts to capture meaning seem, in the very process, to obscure meaning again, leaving money a bit lifeless.

Some ideas from sociology and anthropology

In many ways, sociology and anthropology have more to offer in understanding both the complexity and the subtlety of money attitudes. Money is almost always used interactively: money transactions take place in a 'marketplace', however small the transaction and however private the transaction. The encounter may involve two people, several people or large numbers of people. Or the transaction may take place between a person and a machine. Apart from collectors, who have a particular relationship with money, and others who love to count, or sort their money privately, money is a social substance. It may be easier, therefore, to 'capture' individual money attitudes as they are reflected in action, in transaction. This is precisely how people talk about their money — in relation to others. In this sense, money really is a medium of exchange, if not always of frank exchange.

Viviana Zelizer's work has charted the sort of intermediate territory where the complexity of money, and its underlying social conventions, can be seen clearly.[10] Her book *Pricing the Priceless Child* is a fascinating account of the changing value of children, covering the period from 1870 to 1930 in the United States. Over that time, children changed from being economically useful (even vital) to being economically useless (positively costly), but emotionally priceless. The changing role of children is used to illustrate the larger question of the relationship between economic values and social/cultural values: 'As children became increasingly defined as exclusively emotional and moral assets, their economic roles were not eliminated but transformed; child labor was replaced by child work and child wages with a weekly allowance. A child's new job and income were validated more by educational than economic criteria.' This phenomenon is described in the earlier chapter dealing with current pocket-money practices.

In her later work, Zelizer argues the pressing need for

economics and sociology to come together, to incorporate the 'social and symbolic significance' of money, moving out from the 'theoretical and empirical straitjacket' of the dominant economic paradigm. She describes the way in which circumstances and purposes complicate the picture of money as something that can be regarded as standard and, in economic jargon, 'fungible':

> A $1000 paycheck is not the same money as $1000 stolen from a bank or $1000 borrowed from a friend. And certain monies remain indivisible — an inheritance, for instance, or a wedding gift of money intended for the purchase of a particular type of object. The latter is a qualitative unit that should not be spent partly for a gift and partly for groceries.[11]

This now begins to sound more like the money of everyday experience. American researchers Russell Belk and Melanie Wallendorf also explore some of the ambiguities, inconsistencies and paradoxes of money. They looked at a variety of consumption contexts, including gift-giving, collecting, inheritance, artistic creation, home-decorating, museums and more. Like Zelizer, the authors point out the dichotomy that exists between the economic view of money and the consumer view. In the economic view, money

> has only quantitative meaning. This view may be pragmatic and rigorous, but it fails to offer an understanding of the more emotional, qualitative meanings of money ... In contrast to this view, contemporary consumer society has been characterized as one that often venerates money and imbues it with meaning. Money is revered, feared, worshipped, and treated with the highest respect. Money is, in sociological parlance, considered sacred (Durkheim, 1915). There may be some things that money cannot buy, but even their non-purchasability is cast in doubt when life (e.g. children, surrogate motherhood), death (e.g. contract murder, abortion), love (e.g. bridesprice, prostitution),

prestige (e.g. publicity, political campaigns), and even immortality (e.g. religious contributions, philanthropy) are all bought and sold with money.[12]

The authors' notion of money's sacredness is not religious (though they acknowledge long-standing ties to religion) but rather is based on evidence of the profane nature and uses of money. The authors suggest that positives and negatives co-exist within the realm of the sacred: 'the sacred is extremely powerful ... The simultaneous potential of the sacred to express itself as either beneficent or evil power produces, in the reverent, ambivalent feelings of fascination and repulsion termed kratophany.' Money, too, is a power for both good and evil and elicits similarly ambivalent and contradictory feelings. This was evident from the outset of my research project when people seemed either enthralled or appalled by the topic of money. Fascination and repulsion often go hand in hand.

Anthropologist Mary Douglas explored the part played by ritual in primitive religions, describing the shifting boundaries between purity and impurity, sacredness and profanity. She made this link between ritual and money:

> The metaphor of money admirably sums up what we want to assert of ritual. Money provides a fixed external recognizable sign for what would be confused contradictable operations; ritual makes visible external signs and states. Money mediates transactions; ritual mediates experience, including social experience. Money provides a standard for measuring worth; ritual standardizes situations, and so helps to evaluate them. Money makes a link between the present and the future, so does ritual. The more we reflect on the richness of the metaphor, the more it becomes clear that this is no metaphor. Money is only an extreme and specialized type of ritual ... Money can only perform the role of intensifying economic interaction if the public has faith in it. If faith is shaken, the currency is useless. So too with ritual.[13]

Economists like to make a distinction between modern money, which they describe as 'all-purpose, universal' money, and primitive money, described as 'limited-purpose' money. But modern money isn't always universal and all-purpose, as Zelizer has indicated. Belk and Wallendorf also point out that there are, in practice, many limitations on modern money. It is frowned upon in most Western countries to use money overtly to buy brides or slaves or political office (though it may be used covertly or indirectly for such purposes). We don't accept cheques from some people; cash-only is acceptable for certain transactions (e.g. garage sales, young children's pocket money, illegal drugs). We can't offer money to cancel a social debt, such as a dinner party. The use of modern money is governed as much by social conventions as by economic or prudential concerns.

Gifts of money: an example of psychosocial complexity

There are times, for example, when no amount of money is acceptable. The particularity of money context or purpose is clearly shown in the matter of gift-giving and especially money-as-gift. Research on the subject has shown that money is often considered unsuitable as a gift, and its appropriateness or not depends on complex questions of power, status, intimacy and purpose.[14] Money-gifts can be given to those who are younger, but you can't comfortably give your mother money for her birthday. In many relationships, no amount of money can substitute for a gift personally selected. If people do give money as a gift, the perceived status of the receiver affects the amount people give: if giving money to someone of higher status, people feel they have to give a larger sum than they might spend on a gift. This often applies even without the status differential. It shows money having less 'value' than a gift if more of it is needed. Some researchers have explained the difficulty of money-as-gift by noting the importance of reciprocity — gift-giving creates a bond, or 'debt', in the form of an obligation to reciprocate.[15] People strive to find some sort of equivalence in their gift-giving, but gifts of money are too precise, too explicit, and therefore an imbalance in the exchange may be too visible.

When we do give money as a gift, we often go to great lengths to mitigate the 'coldness' of the gesture, to make it seem special by placing the money in a card or a special envelope. We don't hand over crumpled notes but try to make sure the money looks crisp and new. One of the people I interviewed said: '**When I give a gift, personally selected and wrapped, I don't feel the need to buy a card but prefer to attach a note. But if I give money I feel I must buy a card to "enclose" the money in something I have selected and bought. I feel slightly more comfortable about gift tokens or movie tickets, because they seem a bit more personal.**'

Belk and Wallendorf suggest that 'as a way to perhaps expiate the sacrilege of accepting money for surrogate motherhood, the $10 000 fee in the Baby M case was earmarked by the surrogate mother for the education of her two other children and was not to be spent on more trivial or personal items'. By earmarking the proceeds of a transaction many would regard as dubious, there is an attempt to elevate it from the profane (money for motherhood) to something more sacred (education for children).

So-called 'blood money' involved in the 1998 nurse murder case in Saudi Arabia saved one of the nurses from execution. The Australian brother of the victim exercised his right under Saudi law to receive money in exchange for waiving the death penalty. Clearly no amount of money could compensate for his sister's life and he had earmarked the bulk of it for a hospital in Adelaide, thereby 'sanctifying' the blood money. Later on it emerged that the money had been donated by a British arms company. Profanity! Then the nurses were released and sold their stories to tabloid newspapers, eroding their popular sympathy in Britain. If they had directed the proceeds to charity would it have made a difference?

People tend to think that money is not appropriate for certain transactions, such as gifts, because it is too impersonal. In a sense this is true. The inhibition stems, however, from the fact that money is, in another sense, too personal. Money is so imbued with complicated psychological meanings, meanings held consciously and unconsciously by both giver and receiver — and these meanings may not match — that to give money as a gift is fraught with difficulty. Money can be a token of relative status and worth and this makes it complicated enough in transactions with others. In addition, the memories of money from childhood have shown that our money stories and life stories are linked. Psychological studies confirm their interconnection. We also know that our money attitudes are usually kept secret and that they are a source of negativity and anxiety. Yet we still don't really understand why they should be so negative and so secret.

Money, Freud and Control

There are logical explanations for the widely held negativity and secrecy surrounding personal money attitudes: people may be anxious about taxation compliance, for example; people may have money worries and feel negative; the wealthy may want to be discreet and therefore secretive. But too many questions remain. We saw that negativity is just as likely to come from the well-off as from the poor. Secrecy is as prevalent among the poor as among the rich. Secrecy and negativity transcend income levels.

Why are people so guarded about their financial affairs? Why does it feel like an 'invasion' to be questioned about your personal money? Neither the economic nor even the psychological data provide adequate answers. There seems to be something deeper, and perhaps darker, involved.

Freudian theories about money

American psychoanalyst Sheila Klebanow, writing about money, said: 'Currently, few subscribe to the classical psychoanalytic notion that money equals feces and is, therefore, unclean. But the old concept has many consequences. It is easier to talk about sex than money. Money is too private, too intimate, its personal details far too revealing.'[1]

This refers to Sigmund Freud's 'anal theory' of money.[2] Freud suggested that adult money attitudes were linked to childhood experiences with faeces. The key to Freud's theory is that the child experiences faeces as its first autonomous possession. The young child discovers that it can get a response from its parents (or other adults) by anal retention or elimination, by holding in or letting go (at the right time and in the appropriate place). Parents react with pleasure or displeasure as the child is toilet-trained. Certain potty behaviours may elicit rewards: a smile, a clap, even a material bribe. Or they may elicit anger, disappointment, blandishments and maybe punishments. The child becomes aware that something they autonomously 'own' has the power to influence others' responses, and hence has some ability to control others. This interaction of biological urges with parental responses may then set a pattern, which Freud linked to particular personality characteristics. In Freudian theory, for example, a person fixated at the anal stage of development is likely to manifest the three personality traits of orderliness, parsimony and obstinacy.

An important additional feature of the theory is the erogeneous pleasure that anal retention brings. Withholding is not just a negative matter; there is positive pleasure in retention. Psychoanalyst Otto Fenichel took up Freud's work and related it more specifically to wealth accumulation and to saving habits. He claimed that anal retentive pleasure 'is the erogenous source of the desire for possession for possession's sake and the source of all irrational behavior concerning money'.[3] The pleasure many people obtain from hoarding or collecting connects to this notion of erogeneous pleasure in retention. By contrast, we saw in some of the psychological literature reviewed earlier the suggestion that savers (Freudian anal retentives) are not only parsimonious and obstinate (as Freud himself averred) but also miserable. There was some, though not conclusive, evidence that spenders are happier than savers. In general, however, there is a tendency to underestimate the pleasure that retaining, or saving, may bring to people of retentive disposition.

Either a spender or a saver be

My research suggests that people are predisposed to be either spenders or savers. This echoes the Freudian proposition connecting bowels and booty; people are either basically anal retentive or anal expulsive. Even if not locked into one or other orientation, people are involved in a constant tussle between the opposing urges of holding it in or letting it go. Which gains the upper hand when it comes to money will depend on several factors. The first, and most important, of these is the basic predisposition or orientation developed in early childhood. Other more external or environmental factors will then impact on that basic orientation, encouraging it, locking it in, or discouraging, pushing it in other directions. The level of anxiety people experience about money circumstances is based on the extent to which their predisposition is being threatened or subverted. So a person predisposed to holding in (the saver) will feel far more anxious about encroachments into their nest egg than will someone who basically feels money is for spending, the person who lets it go more easily.

Psychoanalytic theory offers this insight into basic attitudes to money and, in particular, to this predisposition to spend it or save it. Freud said: 'The connections which exist between the two complexes of interest in money and of defaecation, which seem so dissimilar, appear to be the most far-reaching.' Freudian thinking suggests the connection faeces–possessions–savings–money–power. The anal stage of development coincides with the ego-formation phase: 'The original erotic interest in defaecation is, as we know, destined to be extinguished in later years; it is in these years that the interest in money is making its appearance as something new which was unknown in childhood. This makes it easier for the earlier impulse, which is in the process of relinquishing its aim, to be carried over to the new one.'[4]

Control becomes the key to understanding money attitudes. The so-called 'anal character' is identified by the need to withhold and control. Anal retentiveness is most likely to lead to behaviour that puts value on saving. In addition, being by definition a retaining, 'conserving' character, the anal retentive is likely, in psychosocial terms, to be conservative and to retain parents' teaching methods.[5] There is therefore a double layer, as it were, of saving disposition: the early developmental impulse is reinforced by dutiful adherence to parental guidelines. Anal expulsives are also involved in control issues, either directly or in reaction formation. In this case, abandonment of control (or lack of control) is the key, and spending becomes the more likely behavioural outcome.

The urge to spend versus the urge to save is deeply grounded in personal psychology. It is important to stress that the word 'urge' is no accident. Hoarding or splurging, both may be experienced, at some times more consciously than others, as almost irresistible urges. People will say: 'I just need to spend some money; I need to buy something. When I get this feeling I buy a new lipstick/pair of socks/tie.' Someone I sat next to in a dentist's waiting room told me she had felt like spending some money that day so she'd gone out and bought some new hand-towels, adding: 'And then I felt better.' Here was a palpable sense of an urge relieved, a hunger satisfied (or even bowels emptied). Less consciously verbalised is the urgent need to put money aside, the distress felt by some people if they are not building up a nest egg. These spending and saving urges, and individual differences in their application, cannot be explained simply by economic circumstances.

Abnormal and normal money

What all this suggests is that 'normal' money attitudes and behaviours emerge out of childhood, based on the interaction between basic biological urges and parental or environmental experiences. It is often easier to understand the normal by looking more closely at the abnormal. American psychiatrist Edmund Bergler described many money neuroses in *Money and Emotional Conflicts*, a book based on his clinical experiences.[6] He suggests that it begins with infant megalomania — a phenomenon with which new parents are all too familiar. The child assumes it is at the centre of the universe; it feels omnipotent. In normal development, as Freud discovered, this gradually changes as the child adapts to reality. Adaptation involves learning new things about its world as well as overcoming old instincts and patterns, such as this illusion of omnipotence. Bergler asserts that money neurotics may be locked into unconscious, and usually futile, attempts to hang on to childhood omnipotence, to regain the lost paradise of the womb where all needs were automatically, and endlessly, provided.

The paradox of such efforts, however, is that they are often self-defeating. Bergler describes this as 'psychic masochism' — deriving pleasure from pain and disappointment. The 'psychic masochist' collects injustices; unconsciously he is a 'glutton for punishment'. Punishment, moral reproach and guilt bring 'pleasure in pain'. Bergler suggests that this is what leads to much self-defeating financial behaviour. He relates the story of a staid and meticulous accountant who put his own money into a client's 'fly by night' scheme, despite all the warning signs, or perhaps unconsciously attracted by the warning signs. That is, he perversely entered an arrangement that, rationally and professionally, he would have advised his clients to avoid. And predictably it failed. The accountant lost his money, lost his practice, felt humiliated (as he had unconsciously expected, even desired) and eventually sought psychiatric help.

Professional men and women, who do not apparently need the money, often become involved in hopeless money-making ventures, defying all logic. Their behaviour illustrates the element of illogical, infantile, 'wishfulness'. They become 'suckers for easy money', seeking an Aladdin's lamp, a golden egg, a magic puddin', a source of inexhaustible supply. The true money neurotic exhibits aspects of psychic masochism, an unconscious pleasure in disappointment: 'You see, I wasn't meant to make money'; 'I knew the world (mother/father) would let me down and not fulfil my needs'. Bergler says: 'The real battle of money is fought intrapsychically from the reservoirs of unconscious guilt and unconscious defence mechanisms.' Discussing the miser and the spendthrift, for example, Bergler shows just how 'frantic' can be the miser's need to accumulate, and how even the apparently generous 'magic gestures' of the spendthrift may disguise self-denial, a 'psychic masochism' — by giving to someone else, they deny themselves.

Another form of money neurosis is the fear of outdoing parents, or other authority-figure substitutes, such as one's boss. Some people need dependency, seem unable to grasp a sense of themselves as autonomous, independent beings, preferring to let others take the lead. This tendency to devalue themselves, both literally and figuratively, can also lead to self-defeating financial behaviour. Women, in particular, are prone to this sort of psychological attitude. The children, male or female, of rich or successful parents may either strive to outdo the parent or they may fall into this category of self-devaluing neurosis.

Returning to more normal money behaviour, in an economic environment where governments are trying to encourage a higher level of savings, it is instructive to look at money-savers more closely. Saving involves putting money away somewhere, in some form or another, for safekeeping. Sometimes it is just the 'leftovers' that are put away. Sometimes it involves a pre-emptive strike against the pressures to spend, to consume, and the money is put away in advance. Saving involves denial of spending urges, represented by the equation 'saving = not-spending'. It is often based, as described in the discussion of early memories, on attitudes inherited from parents who stressed, and lived, the crucial need to conserve money, to save. Saving was a common theme of most childhoods, and remains a financial mantra of parents today. Yet what makes some people save and others not save, or save less?

Saving levels may have something, though not much, to do with income levels. Lower-income people may have less left in the kitty to save than someone in a higher-income bracket (though even this may be debatable depending on the calls made on that income, the social aspirations and expectations). British research conducted by Adrian Furnham showed that the amount higher-income people saved may be higher than the amount lower-income people saved, but the percentage of money saved per total income was not different. In his study 'Why do people save?', he noted few differences by income level in the saving behaviour and attitude variables he tested. Furthermore, in another study, Furnham found that children's habits of spending or saving of pocket money were established by the age of eight.[7]

Income level is clearly not enough to account for the differences between savers and non-savers. Many parents express surprise and puzzlement about differences among their own offspring in regard to the tendency to be savers or spenders. Even people who were instinctively sceptical and resistant to the basic propositions in this book were halted in their verbal tracks when I asked them about their own children. The tendency of one child to spend, another to save, often bears no relation to parental attitudes, behaviours, prescriptions, nor to external socioeconomic or income factors. 'Why do I have to encourage one of my children to save, the other to spend a bit? They seem to have been born like that.' It is necessary to look more closely at individual psychological predispositions to locate people at one or other point on a saving–spending continuum.

As noted earlier, denial, or saving, is not all about negativity and pain. In her novel *Mansfield Park*, Jane Austen describes as 'an infatuating principle' the pleasurable aspects of saving:

> Having married on a narrower income than she had been used to look forward to, she had, from the first, fancied a very strict line of economy necessary; and what was begun as a matter of prudence, soon grew into a matter of choice, as an object of that needful solicitude, which there were no children to supply. Had there been a family to provide for, Mrs. Norris might never have saved her money; but having no care of that kind, there was nothing to impede her frugality, or lessen the comfort of making a yearly addition to an income which they had never lived up to. Under this infatuating principle ...

An important point about the psychoanalytic perspective is that there can be erotic pleasure in anal retention or its opposite, anal elimination. Psychoanalyst Ernest Jones said: 'Perhaps the most astonishing of all Freud's findings — and certainly the one that has evoked the liveliest incredulity, repugnance, and opposition — was his discovery that certain traits of character may become profoundly modified as the result of sexual excitations experienced by the infant in the region of the anal canal.'[8] Thus there may be pleasure in hoarding money as well as pleasure in splurging money. Scrooge derived pleasure from his own meanness. Indeed, finding the balance between the two extremes (the saving–spending balance) sets up an inevitable tension, which may be experienced negatively or with a frisson of pleasure. Pleasure in saving is captured in this exchange with a patient, reported by Bergler in *Money and Emotional Conflicts*:

A Husband: 'I want you to teach my wife the beauty of thrift.'

Psychiatrist:	'Do you mean the necessity or advisability of thrift?'
Husband:	'Not at all. I mean the beauty of thrift. There is something nice and sentimental about thrift. A dollar is a dollar.'
Psychiatrist:	'That is mathematically correct.'
Husband:	'There is more to it in thrift. Beauty, do you hear me, real beauty ...'

As mentioned in the previous chapter, the *Psychology Today* study conducted by Carin Rubenstein disputed the connection between miserliness and pleasure.[9] The misers on their Midas Scale were more likely to be unhappy, suffer low self-esteem and psychosomatic ailments. A university colleague said of her husband: 'Even if he paid every bill in advance for the next twenty years, he'd still be worrying about the twenty-first year.' This man is a classic anal retentive: he's a map book collector, he's parsimonious and he's reasonably orderly. He recently came into an inheritance, which he is hoarding. 'He just put it into his cheque account, it's not even getting a decent interest rate,' said his exasperated wife. To her it seems irrational, and his behaviour stubborn (and stubbornness is part of the Freudian description). He resists any of her suggestions about putting the money into term deposits. Writing about anal-eroticism, Ernest Jones points out that there are two features of obstinacy: one is to oppose efforts to be told what to do and the other is to resent attempts to thwart conduct already decided upon.[10] The husband has his money where he wants it, and will deal with it as and when he wants to. He ascribes his own cautiousness with money to being a Depression baby. But it goes deeper than socioeconomic factors. Anxiety is never far from the surface for this man, no matter how much money he has. Something will always be threatening his financial peace of mind. This is a highly intelligent, highly educated man. His attitude to money has nothing to do with rationality or income. His worry about future payment of bills is not logical. It clearly illustrates the illogical nature of our relationships with money, an illogic that no amount of money can assuage.

Another person commented that his well-off, elderly mother was becoming increasingly mean with age, as well as increasingly constipated. Though the latter is a common problem for the elderly — exacerbated by medications, poor diet and lack of exercise — the association of meanness with constipation is relevant in the Freudian context. Ernest Jones suggested that the elderly may revert to earlier anal-eroticism as sexual desire or opportunity declines, and may become constipated, mean and irritable. The son felt that his mother's new tightness with money represented a need to assert control over something important, at a time when she was losing control over many other things. At a physical level she was finding difficulty in moving or lifting things without having to ask for help. At a social and emotional level she was no longer being consulted and felt marginalised, ignored, unimportant. Her money, at least, was something she could control, and something she could use, if she chose, to control others.

Exploring age as a variable in studies of saving, British researchers Stephen Lea, Roger Tarpy and Paul Webley note a tendency for the elderly (even well-off elderly) to go on saving in disproportion to their future needs.[11] The desire to leave bequests was not found to be sufficient explanation for this phenomenon. They conclude:

> Simple predictions from psychological data are equally inadequate to explain how saving behavior varies with age. From the experiments on delayed gratification, we should expect children to save very little until the age of 8 or 9, and then to show a gradually increasing ability to save. In fact, young children save much of their pocket money … The disjunction between laboratory results and everyday experience in this area is striking, and deserves further attention.

The tendency for neither young nor old to conform to 'expected' saving behaviours confirms the usefulness of conducting more open-ended research and also validates the insights gained from Freudian theory. In both age groups, the behaviour can be accounted for by the fact that predispositions are evident from an early age and do not go away with increasing age (indeed they may grow stronger).

Baby-talk: keeping money childlike

Underneath the different sorts of money attitudes and behaviours uncovered in this research, I detected some primitive forces at work. This was evident in the stories people told about their early money memories and it will be illustrated again in the three case studies — Elisabeth, Robert and Neil — that follow. Urges to spend or not spend seemed irrational, almost instinctive, but even the talking and thinking about money seemed primitive and childlike. Again, Freud provides a useful conceptual framework for understanding this phenomenon. He drew a distinction between primary process thinking and secondary process thinking.[12] Primary process thinking is dominated by 'the pleasure principle', by instincts and their satisfaction. It is characterised by wishfulness. Secondary process thinking is dominated by 'the reality principle', involves regulation of instincts, and is characterised by thought. It leads, Freud said, to a 'greater delicacy in functioning'. The distinction is particularly relevant to money because a great deal of the language, and the behaviour, surrounding money seems locked into primary infantile responses, into primitive emotions, urges and fantasies.

When the adults in my discussion groups talked about money, especially and perhaps obviously their early money memories, there was a tendency for them to return to a form of 'baby-talk'. Use of diminutives, a plaintive-sounding petulance (for example, when bemoaning their lack of childhood pocket money, or tuckshop money), their continuing sibling resentments, in all of these the language and tone were often childlike. Furthermore, a central feature of adult relationships with money was the way in which attitudes and behaviours involved 'parroting' the earlier generation's attitudes and behaviours. There was an absence of critical, rational reappraisal. Many people simply adopt the parental model, repeating their parents' financial maxims and clichés, which in many cases are no longer relevant. When it comes to money the absence of 'secondary process thinking' is marked. Wishfulness, illogic and fantasy predominate.

In *Childhood and Society*, Erik Erikson set out Eight Ages of Man.[13] The first age he described as 'Basic Trust *v.* Basic Mistrust', and it involves learning to trust oneself as well as others, primarily through feeding, toileting, teething and other infant and early childhood experiences. The quality of this experience, he suggests, forms a basis for the child's sense of identity. He comments that 'even under the most favourable circumstances, this stage seems to introduce into psychic life ... a sense of inner division and universal nostalgia for a paradise forfeited'. The mixture of a need to resolve sometimes contradictory urges and impulses, as well as the nostalgia for an idealised 'perfect' womb-like harmony, are both relevant to money attitudes.

Erikson expressed each of the eight psychosocial ages as opposing polarities; trust versus mistrust or intimacy versus isolation, to give two examples. In each age, there is an inevitable tug and pull between inherently opposite tendencies. This is particularly evident in the second age, which Erikson described as 'Autonomy *v.* Shame and Doubt', when a 'battle for autonomy' takes place, a struggle for a sense of self-control. It occurs at the anal stage of development, a time when the child has two contradictory impulses to deal with — retention versus elimination, to hold on tight or to let go: 'the ratio and sequence of which is of decisive importance both for the development of the individual personality and for that of collective attitudes'. What is fascinating to note in the context of our interest in the devlopment of money attitudes is that the opposite of a sense of autonomy, or self-control, is described as 'shame and doubt'. The implications of this dualism, and the potential for shame, are explored more fully a little later in the book.

Psychoanalytic theory helps to explain many aspects of money attitudes and behaviour, including particularly the propensity to be primarily a saver or a spender, holding in or letting go. This in turn helps to explain why individuals from the same family background can vary in their primary orientation to money and that these variations can be independent of actual income. Erikson maintained that, in order to achieve 'progressive mastery', we need experiences and social reinforcements that help us to develop beyond 'the childish sense of omnipotence which is fed by make-believe and adult deception'.[14] It seems that much adult money-talk and money behaviour is locked into a regressive mode of make-believe and childish fantasy. There is a tendency to baby-talk and to diminution. Elisabeth, in one of the following case studies, refers to 'a little jar' and 'little bankbooks'. Keeping money small keeps it biddable, under control.

Though I did not originally set out on this journey of exploration with Freudian ideas in mind, I kept coming up against aspects and examples of psychoanalytic theories as they emerged unbidden from people in my interviews. But, regardless of whether or not one accepts Freudian propositions, by looking in detail at particular individuals one can see the continuing importance of childhood underlying our adult orientations to money.

Case 1: Elisabeth

Elisabeth was born in Perth and, after leaving school, trained as a nurse. Married with three children, she was part of the middle-income group in my research. When I asked for her earliest money memory she remembered being caught stealing money from her parents' room. She said that she didn't understand what stealing meant until she began to work in her father's business at the age of ten. 'That's when I suddenly understood why it was such a bad thing to do, that you have to earn it.'

In Elisabeth's childhood, the saving message had been conveyed strongly, and she recalled that gifts of cash from relatives were 'whisked away' by her parents to be placed straight into the bank:

'We were taught to save. We had our own little bankbooks, so when we were given money, we saved it. We were also taught that it was hard work, money didn't just fall from the sky. Later on, my sister and I were involved in the family business, and from a very young age we saw where it came from. We were involved in my father paying his staff as well, and then later on I did the books, so it was very much hands-on.

'There's one thing I remember at home: even though my mother was an equal partner, she had her own bank account. That was a real issue, not with my father, but Mum felt she had to have her own economic independence and so she had her own account. I don't. My husband and I have it all jointly, but we discuss things more. My parents tend not to discuss their investments together all that much. They'll talk about it with us children, but together as a couple they tend not to.

'But my father would always say to my mother if she was buying a dress, "Do you really need it? Basically you really don't need it!" It's always stuck, so if I buy something in the supermarket and if it's lollies or biscuits I say, "Well, do we really need them?"'

Elisabeth's comments are rich with detail about relationships, about power and about control. Initiation into an adult world of financial responsibility at a relatively early age seems to have locked Elisabeth into a rigidly dutiful money attitude and behaviour. She carries on her father's prescriptions and, notably, his proscription: 'Do you really need it?' Over her story is the echo of Freudian propositions: that the anal retentive will be dutiful, orderly, and conserve parental values.

It seems hardly surprising that Elisabeth's mother would cling to financial independence in the face of a husband (and then daughter) who uses 'Do you really need it?' to curb her spending. The sort of guilt this may invoke would be likely to encourage furtiveness. It was fascinating to discover later that Elisabeth had her own secret bank account.

In Elisabeth's family, the work ethic and saving were connected and strongly instilled. On the subject of parent expectations she said: '**My father encouraged us to go to uni but he said a degree's only as good as you make it; it's really just a piece of paper unless you can prove yourself. So it's back to initiative, and the bottom line was you can earn $100 000 a year and still end up with nothing. So the important thing was saving, what you did with the money, not how much you made.**'

As a parent, Elisabeth remains committed to passing on the control she has inherited from her father to her own children. At a rational level she sees money as a means to an end: '**It's just a commodity, something that I'd do something with, like buy food or clothes.**' When she stole money, it was to buy lollies '**because the other kids got pocket money and we didn't**'. A little envy had crept in as a motivator (or social comparison as a rationalisation). When asked about any emotions associated with money in the past week, Elisabeth had felt guilt: '**I overcame it quite quickly, but I felt a little bit guilty because I saw something on special and I didn't need it and I thought "Oh well, what the heck" and bought it. And then**

I felt guilty because we've had other expenses that I think take priority. Since I'm not working full time, and the children have started school, I sit back and think, "Well, do I need this extra skirt?" But it was on special anyway, I saved $20 buying it, so you try to rationalise it. Guilt is a true feeling we mums have — it's the idea of the altruistic mother who gives up everything for her children and her husband and goes without. If I had more income, if I was working more hours, I wouldn't hesitate. I didn't feel guilty when I was working more.'

For Elisabeth, the single most important thing her money gives her is security: '**I see it in the long-term perspective, security for myself in my old age.**' Yet she quickly returns to her characteristic theme: '**I make choices, too, not so much from the point of view of "This week we can't afford it", but mainly because biscuits and lollies and lemonade are just lower on the list; we don't need them. I might occasionally buy them for a birthday but, generally, I just make sure the budget doesn't allow for that because I feel we don't need it. I try to keep within a budget and I think of that security of saving for when I'm older.**' This illustrates a different tactic in the control game: a 'rigging' of the budget so that lollies and suchlike are out of the question; a pre-emptive move against temptation.

Elisabeth did not believe it was appropriate to talk about money outside the family, though she felt that 'it's not what people earn that's interesting', but rather what their spending priorities are. Always quick to judge others herself ('Do they really need it?'), she was not keen to be exposed to similar scrutiny. She said that her main priority was her children's education rather than buying an expensive car. She used 'We can't afford it' as a means of countering children's requests and worried that the easy dispensing of modern money (and goods) made control more difficult. Her children are too young as yet for pocket money, but any money they do get is put into 'a little jar'.

Her view of children's household responsibilities illustrated the use of money as a vehicle of control: 'My husband and I made up our minds that the house was a family responsibility and so we wouldn't pay the children for helping with chores. As they get older they'll get a part-time job and if they don't make their own bed or clean their own room, they just have to contribute some money towards me, or whoever.' The notion of children paying their own mother to do housework puts a complex twist on family relations.

Elisabeth likes to use plastic cards for day-to-day money management. The cards serve her need to keep control: 'I've been re-educated by my husband and we tend to use a credit card. But we're very strict: I have to keep all the receipts and check the statement at the end of each month. I didn't feel comfortable with that for a while until I saw the logic of it. If you can pay at the end it's fine and if you're controlled it's fine. I tend to use a debit card with groceries and sometimes a credit card where they will take them. I like to have some cash, but no more than $50 in my wallet. I find that I'm always keeping records now and perhaps I'm better organised, developing different skills because I'm using a credit card more. But you have to keep the records — there have been mistakes and you've been charged for things you haven't bought. We found $200 owing, but you can write and say, "Here are our records". Also, it's just so easy to say "I'll buy that", even though I haven't got the cash on me. You have to be disciplined.'

When people in my focus groups were asked how closely they associated certain items with the word 'money' (the list consisted of eleven items such as notes, coins, credit cards, jewellery, shares and so on), most people put banknotes, coins, cheques and then cards in the top group. Elisabeth was unusual in putting investments, bonds and shares as the three items she most closely associated with the word 'money'. On the surface it seems surprising that anyone should choose these 'non-liquid' items, and also surprising that Elisabeth did not put plastic cards higher up the list.

Elisabeth's response, however, is consistent with the psychological insights we have derived from her responses to general money issues. The items she identified with money are saving items, 'secreted away', illiquid rather than liquid. Retentive. Money, by Elisabeth's definition, is absent, not used. She remains consistently the dutiful daughter, heeding father's advice and being 'sensible' about putting money away. And certainly not frivolous.

Though chosen as representing a middle-income household, Elisabeth self-scored as upper-income, the only person in this research to perceive herself as being in a higher-income group than had been defined for recruiting purposes. This ran counter to the tendency of respondents to self-score towards the middle-income category. Her parents' financial circumstances had improved dramatically during her childhood (or at least this was her impression). She claimed that there was an openness about money, that it was talked about, that she knew her parents' income (her active involvement in the family business has been noted). A financial change-for-the-better does, in general, lead to greater openness in money-talk.

These findings uncovered a childhood Elisabeth, a Daddy's girl dutifully keeping the books. Like an opening balance, this childhood account is carried forward into adulthood, where we see Elisabeth as a dutiful wife, keeping careful credit card records as instructed by her husband. But, like her mother before her, she hides a secret bank account. The guilt, the work ethic and the overwhelming and literal equation of money with control are the keys to understanding Elisabeth's relationship with money.

Case 2: Robert

Robert is a family man who works as an import manager. For Robert, money is primarily about pleasure, about spreading it around rather than holding it in: '**I like to blow it. Living's important but I think it's just as important you get the things with money that bring you some pleasure in life. There's too much doom and gloom out there. I think that if you've got a dollar in your pocket you might as well go out and get what you want and enjoy it while you can. My wife is the opposite. She's got this meticulous little plan that's worked out months ahead. She knows when the heavy bills are due. And she'll count her change at the supermarket. I just shove it in my pocket, think nothing of it. She doesn't waste money. I do. I don't know how much we've got in the bank, I wouldn't have a clue. But I'd struggle without her. She is terrific with money, she budgets very well.**'

This is a wonderful exposition of what 'being good with money' might mean, especially to someone who isn't. To be money-competent, like Robert's wife, involves 'secondary process thinking', as described by Freud. Robert is the antithesis of this; his money-life is full of wish-fulfilling conduct, typifying the psychoanalytic notion of the 'infantile omnipotence fantasy'. He gambles, he doesn't know what's in the bank, doesn't count his change, drops coins.

Robert's early memory of money was of '**how many hundreds of lollies you could get with it**'. Gambling may be Robert's way of trying to recapture the feeling of those 'many hundreds' of goodies in childhood. When responding to a question about the attitudes to money he would like to convey to his own child, he said: '**Well, I'd like him to discover that money's more than the five million toys that are spread around the house everywhere. I'd like him to learn the value of it, that it's one of the key passports to living, surviving, existing. And not so much to protect money, but to be very**

wise. I've been fairly wasteful with money right through my life so far, and I really wouldn't want to push that on. I've got some shocking habits with money. As soon as I see a poker machine I'm gone.'

Exaggerated use of number (hundreds of lollies; five million toys), the pursuit of pleasure and multiplication, wish-fulfilling fantasies — all are themes of Robert's relationship with money. He inherited some of this from his own father: '**Dad was a very generous man. He'd always give you twice as much as you'd asked for. He tends to throw it around; if he's got it you share it.**' Robert's mother, like his wife, was the opposite, stressing that money was hard-earned and should be wisely spent. When Robert was a child his mother sent him to school with his lunch money in a drawstring bag wound around his button. She'd say: '**It's too hard to earn, you can't afford to lose it, or throw it away. Spend it wisely and don't waste it on rubbish — which of course I did.**'

When I asked what irritated him about modern money, Robert was bothered by '**the ugliness money brings out in people at times, the greed, a lot of the violent robberies around**'. At the practical level he is irritated by '**the pesky little $2 coins that don't make a noise when they hit the asphalt. I've lost so many from my pocket since those things were introduced; out with the hanky, out it goes.**' Robert the adult hasn't changed much from Robert the child. He sounds as though he still needs his mother to wind a purse-string round his button.

A research device used in my focus-group discussions (see Appendix) was to ask people to complete a modified 'semantic differential scale' — placing their 'idea of money' somewhere on a continuum (a five-point scale in this case) between opposing pairs of adjectives, such as warm–cold; public–private and so on. Elisabeth responded by ticking the positions around the middle of the adjective pairs. I also asked people to rate various money-associated words (spending, saving, investment, wealth, money, income) on a masculine–feminine continuum. Again, Elisabeth rated most of the items on both scales straight down the middle.

Her responses to these exercises back up the general impression of someone careful and not prone to extremes. Where they are interesting is in contrast with the responses of others. Robert was much more likely to select the extreme positions on the scales than was Elisabeth. There were no 'each-way' bets in Robert's account. For Robert, life and money are exemplified in an 'all or nothing' attitude.

One wonders how this family will fare. Robert's occupation requires that he deal on a daily basis in international currency exchanges, yet he has a weakness for gambling and he loses money from his pocket when he sneezes. His control over money is tenuous. There is a perpetuation of family patterns: the careful, withholding females contrasting with males who can 'let it all hang out'. Fortunately for their finances, Robert says his wife both manages and controls the household money, and he seems, on the surface at least, to appreciate his need for her control.

Case 3: Neil

Neil is a church pastor, married with two children. His early money memory was his childhood practice of saving coins in matchboxes by his bed, away from the prying hands of siblings: '**I remember having a collection of matchboxes on my bed where I used to put my halfpennies and pennies and any threepences I got. It was a saving thing. I used to count them and be pleased about them, locked away from my brothers and sisters.**' Neil is embarrassed to talk about money in case it sounds like '**crying poor**'. Money was never talked about in his own family, though his father was an accountant, but the message about the value of saving was nonetheless conveyed clearly: 'You just knew it was the right thing to do.' His own two children exhibit opposite tendencies: one is a spender, the other a hoarder, so Neil encourages one to save, the other to spend. As parents, he and his wife try to convey to the children that money '**is not the most important thing in the world**', to counteract what they see as undesirably materialistic pressures from friends and media.

For Neil the most important thing money gives is stability: '**It's the sense of knowing where your next meal will come from or knowing you can buy some new plates if you need them. So it gives a stable family life. Probably most of my wife's and my biggest arguments are about money, but when there's enough to cover everything there's a sense of stability because you don't argue about it.**'

Elisabeth talked about her guilt at making an indulgent purchase. Robert recognised his money weaknesses but wasn't much troubled by guilt. Neil talks about guilt, but it's guilt compared with others who have less. He was angered by his son's perception that they were poor, pointing out to him that compared with 90 per cent of the world they are rich. The sense of global compassion leavened some of his more mundane preoccupations about money. Though he was recruited from the lower-income category, he scored himself as 'in between' lower- and middle-income.

In the scaling exercises, Neil opted mostly for the 'somewhat' position: neither in the middle nor at the extremes. One is left with an overriding impression of ambivalence, particularly in contrast with Robert who always played with the extremes. This is not to say that Neil's relationship with money is calm, moderate or feeling 'in balance'. Neil experiences considerable anxiety about money: '**We grew up in different types of families, and that's influenced things. I do the major budgeting and sometimes I have to juggle from this to this to this to make ends meet. I think my wife is a bit befuddled by that or gets annoyed that it happens and often wants to know the**

details but then often doesn't want to know the details. So I sometimes feel betwixt and between, a nightmare to know which way to jump. It's a bit tricky'.

As with his scaling responses, Neil seems a bit 'betwixt and between', as if he really is struggling to know how he feels about money — which way to jump. Use of the word 'nightmare' indicates that money may be quite a serious source of domestic tension.

Like Elisabeth, but unlike most men in his lower-income group, Neil likes plastic money and plastic cards: '**I find them quite useful, credit and debit cards.**' Neil keeps very careful control over his use of ATMs (Automated Teller Machines) and EFTPOS (Electronic Funds Transfer at Point of Sale): '**If I do an EFTPOS or my wife does, I make sure I go straight home and I've got the old budget book and I just deduct it straight from my column that says "food money"; it's gone. I have to do it that way or it would just blow the budget.**' The safety, containment and control of matchboxes by the childhood bed have matured into columns in a budget book performing the same functions.

Neil's psychosocial makeup helps to explain his preference for using plastic cards, which is in contrast to the other lower-income males in my research groups who usually preferred cash. Neil's use is carefully premised upon control, and control is a defining feature of his money behaviour. For Neil the mechanics of money control are probably helping to keep at bay more disturbing aspects of money: at the surface are tensions with his wife about money; beyond this one can sense a resentment of his own lack of money; and, underlying it all, a deep-seated and unresolved anxiety about money and self-control.

These case studies illustrate the way in which individual relationships with money emerge out of psychological predispositions, reinforced by parental admonition and/or example. They expose control as being central to our money lives. The next chapter further demonstrates the centrality of control for all of us — from our wallets and purses through to our relations with banks and to relationships with personal and business partners.

6

Controlling Yourself and Your Money

Money and control are inseparable. When one's money feels out of control, one's life can feel out of control, and vice versa. Money is a powerful symbol of control but also a powerful tool of that control. Controlling money coming in and controlling money going out involves constant readjustment and balancing. Controlling oneself (or not) is the key, and this begins in infancy, as previous chapters have shown. We saw that the psychological wellsprings of our money behaviour run deep. The effects on our money behaviour are always apparent: from everyday management of cash, to weekly budgeting, to spending/saving patterns, to relationships with financial institutions. Controlling others with or through money — the money equals power equation — will be explored in subsequent chapters.

Everyday control and cash

At its most literal, control begins with organising our physical money: the notes, coins, cards and cheques that make up the day-to-day business of money, the mechanics of money. People's attempts to control their everyday money can resemble the marshalling of an unruly primary school football team — the potential for chaos seems always close at hand. There is a feeling that the physicality of money needs somehow to be kept *in control.* Parents feel irritated by their children leaving money 'lying around'. Such irritation goes beyond the untidiness and raises fears in parents that leaving money around, uncontrolled, represents a cavalier attitude to its worth. Some of us pick up small change of little value, such as 5-cent pieces, while others ignore them or sweep them away. A father spoke of his teenage daughters giving him a hug on his return from work in order to frisk him for loose change. The word 'loose' is significant. This is money potentially out of control.

The new Australian currency, both notes and coins, has exacerbated underlying fears about the difficulty of keeping money under control. People complain that the new 2-dollar coins are too small or too light, and that they fall too easily and soundlessly out of pockets, or that the new polymer notes 'spring' unbidden from pockets and wallets. My mother aptly dubbed them 'suicide notes'. A businessman described his tactic of keeping coins in one pocket and handkerchief in the other, so as not to drop one with the other.

The physical form of money is important; people like cash, they care about their currency and they talk about it. They never forget their first pay packet: '**I can remember sitting in my room with money I got from my first pay packet, just looking, touching and counting it.**' People recall the feel, the sound and the smell of crisp new notes, pleasurable sensations usually associated with the old paper money. For adults, the new polymer notes do not have these auditory, tactile and olfactory resonances. No doubt they will provide memories of some sort for younger generations to recall fondly later in life. People's early money stories illustrate the enduring worth of certain childhood coins and notes; adults today often recalling the old threepences, 10-shilling notes and so on.

The majority of people in all the income groups I talked to used an amount of cash each week as the main means of regulating their everyday monetary lives. There is a strong association of cash with food because most households allocate the largest portion of their disposable cash income to regular food shopping. Bills, larger items, one-off, or less regular items may be paid for using a plastic card.

This preference for cash is based on the fact that it is familiar, tangible and controllable. Being 'fungible', as the economists would say, it can be easily allocated (either mentally or literally) for particular purposes. Its use can therefore be monitored. People say cash money feels more 'real' than cards. Expenditure of cash is 'real' and transactions can be *felt* as an exchange of value in a way that does not happen with a card. In this way, cash also acts as a brake on spending. Three women, from lower-, middle- and upper-income levels, describe how this works for them:

'I take out my weekly money, and that's it for the week. Once that's gone it's gone. I prefer to have cash in my purse, then I know I can keep track of it. I can see physically how much is going.'

'When you pay on a card you get the card back so it doesn't feel as if you're really spending. Cash is a more physical thing — you are spending that cash. You hand it over and it's gone.'

'Every week I get out of the bank account what I consider to be my pay, and I budget for the week. I always have cash, although it would probably be more convenient to pay with cards. I think if you're handing over cash you're more aware of what you're actually spending, so you try to be a little more careful.'

My research also indicated that the preference for cash could function as an intra-domestic version of the black economy. Cash is less accountable and therefore more private. By using cash one can avoid the scrutiny of spouses and may avoid the obligation to record-keep, as the following comment shows: **'With the cards there's a record of what you've spent, but I don't like him questioning things so I use cash if I can. I don't like having to make a note every time I spend something. My husband goes mad at me for not keeping track of it. That means you're thinking more about money then, if you have to write it down all the time.'**

So, paradoxically, cash can be more restricting on the one hand, when it is deliberately used as a means of self-regulation, yet on the other hand the anonymity of cash can render it more liberating, less subject to the control of others. Perhaps this points to an additional reason why women may be clinging to cash more than men. Men were less inclined to use actual cash for budgeting purposes, and their daily needs for cash were less. Most men operated with relatively small amounts of cash in their wallets each week (sometimes, in the lower-income groups, the cash was dispensed by their wives).

New technology conveniently serves the preference for cash. ATMs and EFTPOS are regarded by most people as a great benefit, avoiding the need to queue in banks and enabling cash to be obtained easily at all hours, in many locations. Some people take pleasure in the neat dispensation of the notes and the fact that it can feel a bit like winnings — they have to remind themselves that it is actually their own money.

Ready access to cash, however, is not without problems. EFTPOS especially, with its top-ups at the supermarket checkout, can jeopardise careful budgets and erode the 'controlling' benefit of cash. Clearly this has not stopped people from using EFTPOS, but it can be a complicating factor in everyday money lives. The ease with which modern money is obtained does cause unease, particularly in relation to children.

Children think the money is 'just there for the asking', that it comes out of a hole in the bank wall. It potentially undermines the sort of 'seriousness' about money parents are trying to convey to their children, by making it so automatic and accessible:

'I find it harder to teach the children. They're not seeing a bankbook; it's all just coming from nowhere, like magic or something.'

'My kid thinks that money comes from one of those machines on the wall. "Just go to the machine and get some out", an endless supply, like a roll of toilet paper.'

The latter comment, with its Freudian analogy, illustrates the way in which language can unconsciously make connections for us. Many money expressions in common usage demonstrate this, and they are listed in a later chapter.

Despite the general acceptance of machines for withdrawal of money, many people prefer to avoid ATMs for making deposits. There was still a preference for physically handing over cash to a bank teller, knowing that it had reached a safe haven: **'I like to give it to them in their hand and know that they've actually taken it.'** Some people might deposit cheques into an ATM, but most preferred to hand them to a bank teller.

A great change in money management has taken place for the 'mid-age' generation upon which my research focused. Money, for them, has become something like a snack food rather than a main meal, as the following comment from a middle-income man shows: **'When you first start work and you get your first pay packet, you open it up and you've got all these wonderful notes in front of you. And you say, "Well, I've got to put some away for my car, some to live on, some for the disco tonight, and that bit there is going to the bank." You're always going to the bank to put in, to put in, to put in because one day you're going to need it for your house or something of a major capital nature. But now you forever go to the bank to take out. You've got EFT of your salary**

packages, so you're either going into the bank or to the hole in the wall with credit cards. And it's changed the philosophy of your day-to-day life, I think, because you're not sitting down assessing this particular sum that's your salary each week. It's again got this impersonal nature to it — if you need some more money, go and get some. And you drip-feed each time. I don't particularly like it, but that's the way it is, that's technology, that's advances.'

The control of physical money is a marshalling of resources in both a physical and a psychological sense. People vary enormously in the method and the importance they attach to the way their currency is stored. The wallet can become 'sacred' territory because it contains not just our money, which is valuable, but also reveals our idiosyncratic way of organising it. This feels both private and precarious, only just in control. Our wallets are therefore vulnerable to the prying gaze or prying fingers of others, even close family. This helps to explain why a parent may (often reluctantly) give a child permission to take money from their wallet, but hates the child to dally over it, or rifle through it. That begins to feel discomforting, an invasion of privacy. I feel uneasy when my husband 'tampers' with my wallet, even if he is putting money in. It's not that he may not put the notes in the 'right' place; my wallet is not particularly orderly. But it is my disorder, my money. Similarly, the theft of money, particularly from one's wallet, feels like a violation of this intimate, yet precarious, control, which goes well beyond the actual money lost.

Cash, currency and wallets or purses lie on the personal front line of the everyday battle for control. They can exemplify differences between individuals — some people keep their notes in numerical order, in neat serried ranks in the wallet, while others are not troubled by randomness or chaos. Indeed the purse or wallet could provide a sort of archaeological dig-site into personal money attitudes and behaviours.

Similarly, whether people bother to pick up small coins or not, count their change or not, check their bank statements or not, reveals an important set of underlying money orientations.

Control and household spending

Moving outside the management of daily cash and the individual wallet or purse, one comes to the next aspect of money control. This is the balancing act of managing money within the household: balancing the incomings (it is easy to forget that the word 'income' is just that) against the outgoings, and of one person's needs against another's. How organised or formalised a process this will be varies between individuals and among different families. It is basically the crucial matter of budgeting. In a practical sense, for most people this is the allocation of spending: who spends and who decides how much is spent and on what it is spent. The working of this intra-household economy has been much neglected in economic analysis. Jan Pahl's 1989 British research documented the territory in sometimes startling detail.[1] Her work is particularly interesting for the contrasts it reveals between male and female earnings and the relationship to spending within the family.

In most Western countries today, women's earnings make a vital contribution to overall household income. Pahl points out that there is evidence of compensatory balancing — where husbands earn less, wives earn relatively more and vice versa. Though financial reasons come first, an important additional motive for women earning is to gain a sense of independence and self-esteem. The nexus between money and power here is an interesting one. Seventy years ago, in *A Room of One's Own*, Virginia Woolf described the material and emotional benefits of an independent source of income:

> what a change of temper a fixed income will bring about. No force in the world can take from me my five hundred pounds. Food, house and clothing are mine for ever.

> Therefore not merely do effort and labour cease, but also hatred and bitterness. I need not hate any man; he cannot hurt me. I need not flatter any man; he has nothing to give me. So imperceptibly I found myself adopting a new attitude towards the other half of the human race.

Women are protective of their independent earnings. I spoke to several who, though they add most of it into a joint account, nevertheless keep a bit back in another secret account. This 'running away money' is not uncommon: it is a security blanket, a defence against dominant male earning power and the control or lack of independence that it often implies. The most independent women will sometimes rather apologetically confess that in practice they believe 'What's his is ours and what's mine is mine'. Pahl found, however, that wives who saw their earnings as being for the family had more power when making decisions with their husbands as a couple than did wives who saw their earnings as being for themselves. Nonetheless, as Pahl also discovered, there is a discrepancy between theory and practice here. Though both partners tend to define the husband's income as being for the collective, in practice many husbands did not make all their income available to the family. Wives' income, often defined — especially by husbands — as earmarked for wives' personal use, was in practice mostly used to buy things for the family or was added to general housekeeping money.

Another discrepancy uncovered in Pahl's study was the tendency for men to overestimate how much their wives spent on leisure, and for wives to underestimate how much husbands spent on leisure. What emerges from the research is the complexity of links between who earns money, who controls it, who manages it, what is bought, who decides — and the significance of all those interactions. In concluding her chapter on earning and spending, Pahl says:

> Where wives control finances, a higher proportion of household income is likely to be spent on food and

> day-to-day living expenses than is the case where husbands control finances; additional income brought into the household by the wife is more likely to be spent on food than additional money earned by the husband ... These results have important implications for all who are concerned about the living standards of children, about the employment of women, and about tax and social security policies which affect families.

It is this sort of information that has led some governments to direct payment of family allowances to women and not, as in the past, to the (usually) male head of household.

Money and control went hand-in-glove in the responses of the women in my research. Most of those I interviewed were responsible for day-to-day management of household expenditure, the provision of basic needs such as food and clothing, and the payment of routine household bills. The stereotype of women as profligate spenders, requiring men to put the brakes on, was not the impression I gained from my research. Pahl's British findings were similar:

> The extravagant wife, carelessly spending her husband's hard-earned money, appears to be a fading myth, at least by contrast with that other mythical figure, the working class husband whose extravagance endangers the living standards of the family ... he is still alive and still spending money at the expense of his wife and children.

Most of the women I talked to seemed very careful, and often chronically worried, about money. They were faced with the everyday reality of the costs of routine living in a way that many of their husbands were not. Keeping control of money was a daily, constant issue: how to eke out the weekly budget to satisfy family needs, pay essential bills, enable some pleasures and allow for unexpected costs. This was their money world. It was especially true for women in the lower- and middle-income groups because controlling money was coupled with a more pressing anxiety about not having enough for the basics. For all these women, resisting pressures to consume more, or the temptation to spend impulsively, were daily issues in a way that was not true for many of the men I interviewed.

As we have seen, for routine budgeting and spending, most people withdraw a regular amount of cash each week in order to control the money they allow 'out'. If they don't use cash they may use cheques or cards. But the purpose is the same. This is the best way to keep the spending of money *under control*. 'When "big money" is hard to control, small amounts assume greater significance,' says Australian social researcher Hugh Mackay.[2] Supriya Singh, who looked at money in marriage in Australia, noted the continuing importance of cash and the tendency to the 'jam jar' mentality in allocating amounts of money for particular activities or needs.[3]

Whatever the tactics adopted, the underlying purpose of all this is strategic control of money and, particularly, control of spending. We each have a personal 'system' to achieve this end, more or less organised, more or less conscious, and more or less matched with that of our domestic and business partners. At the moment, many personal money control systems are in a state of flux, and sometimes disarray, because traditional household budgeting systems have come under pressure from technological change. People haven't yet adjusted to the new ease of money access. ATMs and EFTPOS, by enabling (even causing) frequent top-ups to what was once a weekly or fortnightly cash budget, show that money may come more easily, but control may get harder. Money systems will continue to change, probably with even greater rapidity, but the underlying issue of control will remain.

Spending money may be impulsive, in which case the pleasure is sometimes tempered by feelings of guilt. Usually, however, spending involves a degree of planning and seems rational (though it may not be). Financial planning, in some form or other, is essential for most families. It leads to the feeling, expressed often in my research, that people 'resent' the amount of mental time and space that money occupies: **'There is too much thinking about it'**; **'I wish we didn't have to think about it so much'**. These are other ways of saying: 'I wish we didn't have to control it so much; I wish we could just let it go.' Lower-income people assume that it is because their income is low that they are so preoccupied by it. But upper-income people are equally preoccupied. The issue of control is the same.

Control over one's money is a precarious business and is easily threatened. This was apparent in many of my interviews when people raised the issue of privatisation. Like many governments around the world, several Australian State governments have set about privatising previously government-owned utilities and services. In talking about personal money and household management, many people expressed concern about this policy. Decisions made by politicians, affecting areas that are fundamental both to wellbeing and to household budgets (such as electricity, water and local government services), have the capacity to undermine barely controlled financial lives. The outrage expressed by some interviewees was as much about loss of control as it was about changing costs: 'For those who have lost control over their money, money cannot represent a set of neutral symbols … rather money is fraught with trouble, entailing a sense of anxiety in dealing with it.'[4]

Control and banking

The interface between the individual and their bank provides another manifestation of money and control. The links between early memories and childhood experiences with money, as well as the importance of the predispositions uncovered in the previous chapter, help to explain much that is puzzling about our relationships with banks. There is ample evidence, as we have seen, that money has a childhood history and that its 'value' is not only quantitative. Money incorporates parental struggles, aspirations and exhortations. This emotional currency renders money more complex than financial institutions realise, and probably more complex than we understand ourselves.

This is the context within which we conduct our financial affairs, influenced by the constant underlying issue of control. This is one woman's reaction to banking through ATMs: **'I'm against the principle of it. I mean that's what banking's for: to give you service. And I really like going in and saying, "I'll have five $50s and two $20s". I like my own denominations, and I like the security of being inside a bank when I get money. I put it in my purse, it goes in my handbag, and then I walk out of the bank.'**

The response illustrates the assertion of money control on several fronts: choosing her own note configurations; getting others to do her bidding; orderly control of the physical cash; and controlling the safety of her environment. Similarly, keeping control of money underpins the preference of those who continue to make bank deposits into the hands of a human teller rather than an ATM. It feels more in control, less likely to disappear into the unknown: **'I don't quite trust it in the machine — I prefer to place my money in human hands for safekeeping.'**

Parental fears that children take money for granted, or spend it too easily, are exacerbated by newer banking technology. Much of the apparent concern about children's spending propensity, however, is a projection of concern about ourselves. Many people are hanging on to personal exchange at bank counters because they fear the ease with which the money comes (and goes) when accessed through ATMs. One man said he preferred not to use ATMs at all: **'It's too direct. I don't want to feel responsible for my money, I want the bank to be responsible. It's too easy — I get worried when I go to an ATM that I might just take it all out!'**

This man wants something to act as a go-between,

someone to mediate his basic urges. A machine won't do. Subconsciously, he wants a parent substitute, to be pleased when he puts money in, displeased when he takes it out. Above all, he wants someone to protect him from himself. So he uses, and expects, the bank (in the person of a teller) to do this for him. A machine is too easy, too nonjudgemental, too 'unserious', for this man and his money. He prefers to retain a sense of the bank filtering his impulses, forcing him to keep control. It is yet another example of the way in which control permeates the relationship between individuals and the everyday banking process. It demonstrates again that our money behaviour is characterised by irrational as much as rational impulses.

Control affects the banking relationship in a more symbolic sense as well. People need their banks and yet they feel angry with the banks a lot of the time. This anger often seems out of proportion to the particular issue, whether it be bank fees or cheque clearance times or whatever. The anger is connected to the question 'Who is in control here?' In 1988, the then State Bank of Victoria ran an advertising campaign containing the line 'It's *your* money Ralph'. This is often quoted, a decade later, when people want to illustrate their need to assert control in their dealings with banks. The advertising refrain tapped a need to remind ourselves that we are in control, however tenuous this may seem at times. Similarly, when people talk about the need to 'educate themselves' about money, they imagine that by being informed they can reassert control. In both instances, this is as much a dialogue with self as it is a dialogue with the bank.

In the routine to-and-fro of running a life, a job and a household, the actual 'in and out' of money takes place via the banking system. Thus guilt about spending, about not saving, may be projected onto the bank. This renders the relationship fraught from the outset, the bank psychologically taking the place of a disapproving parent, usually father. Even people who think they want the bank to mediate their responsibility, to keep them in line, nevertheless may, at the same time, resent that very dependence. In the next chapter we will explore questions of dependency and resentment more fully through the contribution of psychoanalyst Melanie Klein.

In this context, it is also easier to understand why so many people do prefer ATMs and EFTPOS, especially for withdrawing money. Now that salaries and other payments are often made by direct transfer into personal accounts, everyday banking transactions are mostly withdrawals rather than deposits. The depersonalisation of these transactions may be an advantage: not only do they offer privacy but, importantly, machines don't make judgements. Images of the parent, all those childhood admonitions to save, may be carried in one's mental bankbook. A human interface can enliven this mental image in a way that is less likely with a machine. In practice, the bank teller is usually indifferent to our routine financial transactions, and the impersonal attitude of a real person can be more galling than that of a machine. Many people have been pleased to switch to machines and rid themselves altogether of any remaining sense of the bank as father-figure restraining their impulses.

There is a larger issue in relation to banking upon which most comment focuses. This is the question of control and its relationship with power. Banks are seen as large, powerful, uncontrollable institutions, with power over individuals and families, and possessing substantial political clout.[5] The fact that most debate centres on these aspects of banking is perhaps what causes the sense of helplessness sometimes experienced by the ordinary person. His or her relationship to the bank takes place at an intersection between personal, subjective money and official, objective money. The world of banking, however, is fronted by imposing head offices, imposingly paid head officers and imposing profits (even in bad times). It speaks a language vastly different from that of the personal experience of money. The result is not only inequality but also incomprehension. This underpins feelings of helplessness and powerlessness that in turn fuel frustration, anger and resentment.

The spending–saving seesaw

For most of our money-lives we try to strike the right balance between spending and saving. Finding the balance begins within the individual, and it is here that we saw the importance of psychological predispositions. Almost everyone I talked to directly or inadvertently revealed these predispositions. The three case studies presented in the previous chapter — Elisabeth, Robert and Neil — demonstrated this most clearly. People find they are basically either a spender or a saver, or somewhere between the two on a continuum. This affects their money behaviour, and the emotions associated with that behaviour, probably for their lifetime. Other factors will impinge and alter the emphasis but, whether followed or reacted against, predispositions have a continuing impact. Some people explicitly recognised the innateness of their saving–spending position: '**It's bred into me. I can't help it.**' '**I've always been interested in keeping, in saving.**'

An individual predisposed to saving cannot simply burrow into that predisposition: he or she is constantly under pressure to spend, and needs to find a way to deal with that pressure. The passion of resistance is evident when such a person says with great emphasis: '**I hate spending money.**' The saving predisposition is, often of necessity, a defensive position. People do not say 'I love saving', but rather that they hate spending. People do not like to seem mean, though there is some ambiguity inherent in Protestant attitudes when excessive saving may be seen as mean while thrift may be regarded as a virtue. In *The Individual in the Economy* the authors suggest that a 'pseudomorality' of saving serves the purpose of constraining excessive spending by making saving 'moral'.[6] They make the point that saving, as a primary goal in itself, is often disguised or denied. Thus, to be a Scrooge may remain a private affair, and this in itself lends some support to the association of money, especially the retention of money, with something potentially shaming.

As discussed in the previous chapter, it is important to recognise that the saving position is not all negative, though it may remain secretive. There can be positive pleasure in saving, in hoarding, in '**knowing you have a nest egg**', '**in seeing it grow**'. We have seen how psychiatrist Edmund Bergler discussed the 'beauty of thrift'; economist J.M. Keynes referred to an 'instinct of pure miserliness'; and novelist Jane Austen described as an 'infatuating principle' a character's pleasure in seeing money safely put aside, in watching it grow, almost in consolation for her childlessness.[7] All describe a pleasurable sensation attached to saving that goes beyond mere prudence or necessity. Generally speaking, however, the pleasure of saving does tend to remain private.

It is different for spenders: they will say, '**I just love spending money.**' They describe a 'hit', a 'buzz' or a 'rush' associated with spending that is explicitly pleasurable. One man, commenting on the pleasure of spending, went on to say: '**I'm probably not very well controlled. I think I always spend too much. Maybe when the kids get older and there are more expenses I'll have to be a bit more contained.**' Spenders enjoy seeming generous (though they may worry about seeming irresponsible, profligate or advantage being taken). Display and emulation are external and explicit, albeit in varying degrees, compared with the more inwardly-turned saving position. As long ago as 1899, Thorstein Veblen coined the phrase 'conspicuous consumption', its adoption in common currency acknowledging this irrepressible partnership.[8]

Like the savers, however, spenders may not get free rein. They must contain their urge and restrict their pleasure in the face of external constraints: personal, social and economic. In general, both savers and spenders face a constant struggle — more or less painful depending on circumstances — to find a balance within themselves between saving and spending. Many people I talked to about their spending patterns mentioned their tendency not to spend and then suddenly to spend a lot, or buy several items at once — 'to go on a spending spree'. Rather than fitting a rational pattern of saving in order to spend, this behaviour often sounds more like an eating disorder, bulimic in its intensity. The gastrointestinal metaphor parallels the psychoanalytic theory: Freudians at one end of the alimentary tract, Kleinians at the other (as we will discuss in the following chapter). The 'splurging' phenomenon seems sensual or peristaltic rather than rational or irrational. It reveals pleasure in retention followed by a sudden rush of spending, an opening of the floodgates, an almost uncontrollable release. Though pleasurable at the time, this behaviour sometimes causes much guilt, illustrating Bergler's description of 'psychic masochism'.

In between the savers and the spenders are those for whom money remains 'a commodity', simply a vehicle for spending or saving: '**Money is just a tool you get from work; it's something you exchange for other things of value.**' '**You work for it, you get it, you do something else with it.**' Such people claim that the use of money in itself does not bring pleasure or pain; it is only the object purchased or the amount achieved that gives pleasure. For these few, money comes close to being the neutral medium of exchange described in economics texts. In my research, they were a minority. They remain, however, psychologically predisposed to spend or save. Indeed, precisely because they hold to the view of money-as-commodity, they seem to resent more deeply any intrusion of emotion into their relationship with money. It is supposed to be neutral and yet it is causing worry. Objective money becomes subjective: '**I resent the feeling that I have any anxiety about money because I don't think you should and I don't like it**'.

As each individual struggles within themselves to find and maintain an equilibrium between spending and saving, a second level of saving–spending balance has to be found within each household. Adults come into a household unit, as into a business partnership, carrying the baggage of their own internal predispositions, as well as more specific attitudes and experiences acquired from their parents. The Latin word for baggage, *impedimenta*, conveys the sense in which this baggage can be an impediment to the free play of money exchange in adulthood. For only a few individuals does money come near to being a neutral commodity. For most its use is complicated by a host of irrational factors of which most of us remain unaware.

Household partners have to contend with finding individual and complementary balances at the same time as they have to deal with ever-changing external pressures. In his book *The Market Experience*, political psychologist Robert Lane points out that models of economic rationality, based on a straightforward idea of maximising utility, are of limited value when we look closely at individuals (or households).[9] The balancing adjustments are constant. One person I interviewed used a seesaw analogy in which the balance sometimes tips too far (usually towards the spending end of the seesaw). The level of anxiety caused depends on circumstances and, more importantly, on the personal predisposition to be a saver or a spender. A saver will be much more unsettled by running down a cash-cushion than someone who is a spender.

Couples may complement each other in their financial dispositions — one partner a saver, the other a spender. Brakes and accelerators. Contrary to popular belief, brakes are not necessarily male, and accelerators are not necessarily female. Such differing, but complementary, money styles were captured in the following comment: '**To me money's a detail; for her it's something that's very specific. If we went to a supermarket she would count her change. I'd put the change in my pocket and say, "It'll probably be alright".**'

The following diagram 'Personal money attitudes' sets out this interactive picture: internal predispositions, unconsciously formed in early childhood, are reinforced (or reacted against) under parental influences over the ensuing years into young adulthood. The three main aspects of this more conscious level of parental influence are: the atmosphere surrounding money (unspoken messages such as silence and prudence); specific (spoken) admonitions and maxims about money; and money action (behaviour observed and experienced by the child). From this the individual develops a propensity to be primarily a saver or a spender, the key variable involved being control. Anxiety levels reflect the extent to which the predisposition and the sense of control feel under threat. Predispositions may also have a bearing on other personality variables such as optimism, externality, self-esteem, competence, efficacy and so on. These, in turn, affect outcomes in the saving–spending balancing act.

As we have said, each individual takes their predisposition into relationships with others, as well as into the broader social and economic environment. Interactions with marriage and business partners, and with one's own children, are affected by the combination of internal predispositions and external experiences, and may in turn be influenced by the perceived pressure from the next generation's needs and wants.

In a general sense, the unconscious predispositions remain open to mediating influences. American researchers Paul Wernimont and Susan Fitzpatrick suggested that money can be a learned value, noting the effect of particular working environments on money attributes such as secrecy.[10] However, predispositions are as likely to influence job preferences, and hence working environments, as they are to influence money attitudes. Life-orientation and money-orientation are linked. The sort of person who opts for an occupation or work environment that stresses 'conservative business values', such as secrecy, is quite likely to be an anal retentive, valuing orderliness, and

Personal money attitudes: inputs and outcomes

How we each arrived at the saving–spending position

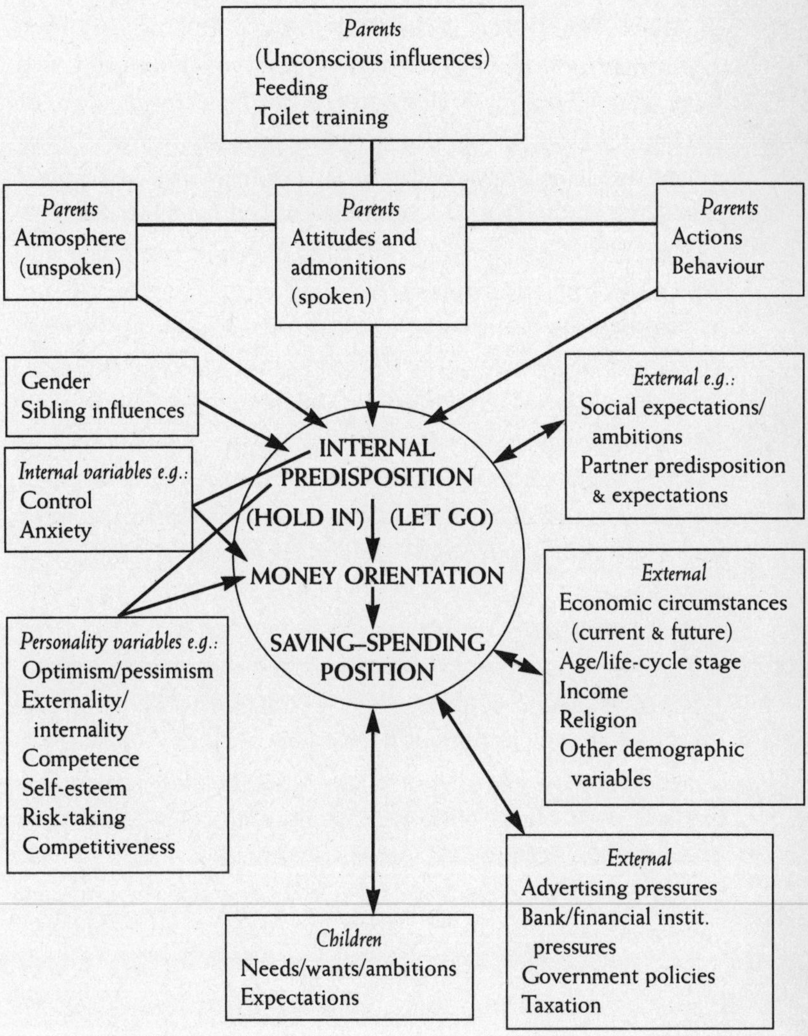

parsimony, and with a tendency to follow parental (and therefore organisational) prescriptions and norms.

Nevertheless, it is also likely that the choice of a marriage or business partner may affect the extent to which one's predisposition can be played out. In reference to the three detailed case studies in Chapter 5, someone married to Robert, for example, would need to play the role of brake rather than accelerator, regardless of their own predisposition, if the marriage were to be financially viable. That person's tolerance of the role they may be obliged to play will in turn depend on the extent to which it sits comfortably with their own predisposition. Part of the ongoing business of 'finding the balance' is likely to involve constant adjustments and readjustments, depending on circumstances.

Finding the balance between competing forces first within each individual, then within the couple, then in external economic interactions, and then within government and social priorities, is a delicate and difficult business. The balance of external factors also changes with time and circumstance. In countries suffering hyperinflation, for example, money's financial value decreases so rapidly that there is no point in saving it unless it can be shifted elsewhere. British research by Adrian Furnham showed that optimism about the future is an important personality (internal) and environmental (external) variable when it comes to saving or spending money.[11] Nevertheless, the important psychological orientation to be a saver or a spender, a brake or an accelerator, remains. The pleasure *and* the pain attached to spending *and* to saving need to find their way into our economic equations.

7

Of Milk and Money

Predispositions are not the whole story in the formation of our attitudes to money, but they are almost certainly the start of it. This is confirmed by another psychoanalytic perspective on money attitudes — that of Melanie Klein. Her theories provide an important link with questions of money and power, and are especially fascinating in their exploration of issues surrounding wealth and inheritance.

Putting your money where your mouth is

Melanie Klein located money-attitude development at an earlier stage in infancy than did Freud.[1] Klein described the 'phantasy of an inexhaustible breast', linking hunger for money to the notion of never-ending nourishment: the infant feeds automatically in the womb and, for a short time after birth, it moves from this all-encompassing nurture to a sense of itself being as one with its mother: 'Under the dominance of oral impulses, the breast is instinctively felt to be the source of nourishment and therefore, in a deeper sense, of life itself.' However, the infant inevitably experiences delays and frustrations to the constancy of the milk supply, whether breast or bottle, and begins to sense that there is a difference between self and non-self. Klein suggests that some frustration may be necessary to the child's developing sense of competence.

Too much frustration, however, can fuel a fantasy of inexhaustible supply that may later be translated into an insatiable hunger for money. The fact that it is insatiable helps to explain why some very wealthy people never seem to be satisfied; they are driven to continue the quest, to always have more. American writer Thomas Wiseman describes as 'nirvana nostalgia' the efforts made by some millionaires, in luxury penthouses, to 'recreate that imaginary condition of total isolation and total safety and comfort of the womb ... Instant gratification is the order of the day. In this luxury cocoon, they have created an artificial inexhaustible breast, and feel safe.'[2]

As the infant begins to sense a difference between self and non-self, Klein says it makes a perceptual distinction, or split, between the 'good breast' that is satisfying, and the 'bad breast' that is frustrating. The good breast gets idealised and endowed with magical qualities. But there is an ambivalence here that may underpin some of the awkwardness about riches so evident in my interviews. In his journal article intriguingly titled 'Mr. Moneybags Meets the Rat Man: Marx and Freud on the Meaning of Money', E.V. Wolfenstein says: 'in the shape of the ideal breast we find the ultimate emotional foundation of the mystery of money, of its false promise of happiness.'[3]

The notion of 'false promise' is what may lead to anger and envy. This is an important element of the Kleinian contribution. She uncovered the paradox that there can be resentment of 'the very ease with which the milk comes'. As Wiseman puts it: 'This seemingly inexplicable phenomenon is accounted for in the Kleinian concept of envy. According to this, we envy that which does us good for the goodness that it is capable of doing.' He points out that the idea of resentful envy helps to explain the fact that generosity very often invokes ingratitude. This is particularly obvious in maternal–child relations when the self-sacrificing actions of a mother are both welcomed and resented. It is also obvious in money relations, when the fact that one is dependent on another for income may produce simultaneous gratitude and resentment.

Examples of Kleinian ideas emerged frequently in my research. It has already been noted that some people fear and resent the ease with which money flows from ATMs. One woman, with an annual income of $750 000, was furious about minor bank fees of $7 on one of her accounts. It's not a matter of wealth or amounts, but it is about resentment of dependency. People like to tear banks down, metaphorically, to devalue the source; a very Kleinian precept. (The banks, however, would have difficulty accepting that they may be seen unconsciously as 'bad breasts'!)

When wealthy people feel compelled to become involved in philanthropic works, their compulsion to give money away is linked to an ambivalence about riches, to anger and resentment, especially when the source of that wealth is inheritance. To give it away is to thumb a nose at the controlling power of the source. As Klein puts it: 'To "bite the hand which feeds one" … is almost synonymous with biting, destroying, and spoiling the breast.' When one listens to the wealthy discussing their early money memories, the controlling power of money is both apparent and resented: '**My earliest memory is of my grandfather being overly generous with everyone, throwing it around, which was sort of offensive because he used it to control us. We had to love him, had to come running and sucking up to him because he was giving it to us.**'

'Sucking up'? Even the language of money in common use connects with the Kleinian concept of milky nourishment. We refer to 'the cash cow' and 'milking the cash cow'. To be living in the 'lap of luxury' connects motherhood and riches. When people talk about money, especially in relation to their early memories, there is strong association with food, particularly 'special' foods, indulgences and treats. Some recollections also included descriptions of a mother's purse that had the quality of an idealised 'good breast'. For example: **'It was my mother's purse that I remembered. We'd be out and she'd be always opening it and taking stuff out and buying things, a lolly or two. That's my recollection, getting something via the purse, this magical thing that gave you things.'**

Edmund Bergler's *Money and Emotional Conflicts* contains this comment about miserliness:

> Now, there is only *one* situation in life in which pennies, nickels, and dimes were of prime importance, and that situation is early childhood. Many a millionaire parts much more readily with one-hundred-dollar bills than he does with his dimes. And there's a reason for this: in the *pre*conscious, the penny, the nickel, and the dime have the emotional value of sweets, chewing gum, and ice-cream sodas. *Un*consciously, the coins have the emotional value of money stolen from mother's purse — the whole infantile pseudo-aggressive defensive conflict in miniature.[4]

We all know people like this, especially wealthier ones: people who easily spend large amounts of money but who complain and quibble over small amounts. Echoing Bergler's description, a wealthy interviewee said to me: **'One of my earliest memories was my parents arguing over money, because my father was a control freak. Money was power to him and he really used it. I remember us being very comfortable and money not being an issue, but it was a niggle in the family, and I'd pinch money from my mother's purse because I was never allowed money for the tuckshop.'**

Several people in my research continued feeling guilty in adulthood about stealing from their mothers' purses. Their adult justifications often contained a sense of 'getting their own back' (biting the hand that feeds) for not being given any, or enough, pocket money or tuckshop money; the inexhaustible supply being frustrated or denied: '**I was aware that our family was pretty rich, but there wasn't much money around other than what was in Mum's purse. I think I occasionally stole money from Mum's purse, and I still feel wicked about that.**' Klein suggests that 'one of the deepest sources of guilt is always linked with the envy of the feeding breast, and with the feeling of having spoilt its goodness by envious attacks'.

My research indicated that it was the wealthy in particular who talked about money in terms that often reflected Kleinian ideas. One woman maintained that to discuss money at all was 'too close to the chest'. There were other instances of the 'milk and flow' metaphors emerging spontaneously in money discussions: '**I suppose as I get older I'm more conscious of the things that as a family we take for granted. We're all able to get food and so on. On the other hand, I suppose it's a paradox; I also say to my children that the source of our wealth is still largely with the family business and that may not last. The great big tit might dry up.**'

A young wealthy woman, talking about inheritance, said: '**I don't want to be reliant on someone dropping it on me from heaven. I think my cousins will just spend it — here it is, we'll buy some milk, go and drink it all and it's gone. Then they have to wait for more to be given to them. I'd rather be controlling it myself than having to rely on someone else controlling me.**'

The comment illustrates several major themes, especially the resentment of ease and the operation of control. Some of us might think of champagne as the appropriate rich person's elixir, but the reference to milk in the inheritance story illustrates the ability of language to reveal unconscious pathways of the mind.

The psychoanalytic perspective on money locates the development of money attitudes firmly in early childhood. We now begin to understand why personal money can be so perplexing — money attitudes are formed around intimate relationships and situations. Here are the seeds of the fierce privacy with which many people guard their money affairs, the awkwardness and the secrecy. Money as taboo is now more understandable, though this may be largely unconscious. This psychoanalytic insight can explain the negativity, tension and anxiety, but it can also explain the pleasure. These are the origins of the essential ambivalence that characterises our relationship with money.

Money prudery

Discussing the setting of patients' fees, Freud said:

> The analyst does not dispute that money is to be regarded first and foremost as the means by which life is supported and power is obtained, but he maintains that, besides this, powerful sexual factors are involved in the value set upon it; he may expect, therefore, that money questions will be treated by cultured people in the same manner as sexual matters, with the same inconsistency, prudishness and hypocrisy.[5]

Sexual aspects of money contribute another layer to the awkwardness and the reticence. People say that talking about money to their children can be as difficult as discussing sex. In a recent newspaper report a television commentator, reflecting on her childhood, said: 'I was brought up with a chauvinistic father. We didn't talk about sex or money. They were both dirty words, so I never learnt where money or babies came from.'[6] Freud used the word 'prudishness'. Most of the psychotherapists writing about money today still refer to money prudishness and sexual prudishness, often adding that sexual prudishness has all but disappeared, at least in the consulting rooms, whereas money prudishness continues. There is reference to a 'fiscal blindspot' in therapy, where both therapist and patient avoid the subject of money in general, and of fees in particular.[7]

Personal money is veiled with a certain prudishness, as we have already observed. To describe someone as 'of modest means' shows the power of colloquial expressions to encapsulate some of the subtleties of money. Financial modesty is demanded of children of the wealthy, illustrated by the use of slightly coy-sounding euphemisms to describe richness — the wealthy women in my research used the expression 'having a wealth base' rather than calling themselves 'rich' or 'wealthy'. They would probably defend this as a more accurate description of the varied circumstances that gave them the credentials to join the groups. The circumspectness, however, has a flavour both of avoiding the potential 'filthiness' of riches as well as of being suitably demure.

The association of money with cash and cash with payment for 'dodgy' or fringe economic activity reinforces silence and prudery. In an interview, novelist Thomas Keneally described the useful intermediary role of literary agents, saying: 'The writer can be a high-class tart — they don't ever have to mention money.'[8] Cash transactions often take place at the nether end of the economic chain of respectability: prostitution, pawn shops, tax dodging, low-skill, low-pay. German philosopher Georg Simmel, discussing payment for prostitution, says: 'The relationship is more completely dissolved and more radically terminated by payment of money than by the gift of a specific object, which always, through its content, its choice and its use, retains an element of the person who has given it.'[9] In the recent Booker prizewinning novel *The God of Small Things*, Arundhati Roy describes the payment of fees for prostitution: 'a fee *clarified* things. Disjuncted sex from love. Needs from Feelings.'[10]

The use of money to achieve closure, and to buy impersonality, was illustrated in writer Helen Garner's experience of a masseur who flouted professionalism by suddenly kissing her during a session. Instead of refusing to pay in protest, or hitting him, or walking out, she meekly paid the bill. As she said in a later radio interview, the act of payment was 'to complete the transaction ... as if nothing had happened'. In other words, to wipe it out. Simmel described this liberating aspect of money quantification, enabling emotional disengagement.[11] Use of money in this way is also reminiscent of Bergler's description of the 'magic gesture'.

Ambivalent and secretive attitudes to money are captured in a passage from David Lodge's novel *Therapy* in which the narrator has just visited his acupuncturist:

> I left her cheque in a plain brown envelope on the little table where she keeps her needles and other stuff. The first time she treated me I made the mistake of taking out my wallet and crassly thrusting banknotes into her hand. She was very embarrassed, and so was I when I perceived my faux pas. Paying therapists is always a bit tricky. Alexandra [his analyst] prefers to do it all by mail. Amy told me that on the last Friday of every month when she goes into Karl Kiss's consulting room there's a little envelope on the couch with her bill in it. She picks it up and silently secretes it in her handbag. It is never referred to by either of them. It's not surprising, really, this reticence. Healing shouldn't be a financial transaction — Jesus didn't charge for miracles.[12]

This is money operating in borderline territory, when private money has to cross into commercial territory and finds itself floundering; territory we explored in relation to pocket money. Certain activities or services are deemed, consciously or unconsciously, to be out of the acceptable purview of monetary exchange. Like mother's milk, the healing professions are one such area. Researchers such as Belk and Wallendorf point to the use of mediators to mask the awkwardness: the doctor's receptionist handles the bills, separating the service from the money and so preserving 'the altruistic, aesthetic, or sacred interpretation of the service-giver's actions'.[13]

Payment for other domestic or personal services, such as to

plumbers, gardeners or dentists, may not be quite such an affront to these notions. When transactions involve us paying the person directly, however, there may be enough awkwardness to feel the need to fold the cheque over or to put money in an envelope. Similarly, gifts of money need to be mitigated by placing them in a card, or special envelope, or inclusion with something else. This keeps it personal while keeping it covered, modest, less crass, less exposing and exposed.

In the Helen Garner episode, money was used to de-personalise an exchange that became too personal. Payment of money removed the sexuality, rendered it impotent. One of the people in my research groups told of buying herself expensive clothes on her husband's credit card to 'pay him back' for having an affair with another woman. Money in this case was used to inflict punishment, to make herself heard, to feel less impotent. People talk about 'therapeutic shopping' designed to give themselves 'a lift', the pleasure coming from the act of spending as much as from the actual object purchased. Revenge shopping, however, is designed to draw attention and to punish. In the Garner example, money is used to de-personalise, in the other example to personalise. In both cases, however, money is being used to punish an offender and to re-empower the self: a powerful medium of psychosexual exchange.

Prurience: the other side of the coin

The partner of prudishness is prurience. An almost voyeuristic fascination with money was evident throughout my research as people reacted to the topic. Will she reveal all? There was immense curiosity, a fascination with the forbidden. The desire to peek into others' wallets, figuratively or even literally, resembles the fascination with others' sexual habits. Exactly how do other people organise their money? What are the precise financial arrangements of one's friends? On the whole, we don't know and, on the whole, we certainly would not ask. It is considered 'indelicate' to ask and equally 'indelicate' to tell. But we'd love to know!

Jan Pahl's British research into the intra-household economy demonstrates how unwise it is to treat 'households' as if they were an undifferentiated unit. She reveals that there is 'her' version and 'his' version both of the marriage and of money in the marriage, and these versions often differ. Within marriage there are secrets, money matters not discussed, not confronted. Pahl also notes 'the astonishment' expressed at other people's financial arrangements when they are revealed.[14] One person, after describing her own financial arrangement with her husband, said: 'it puzzles me that most of our friends in similar circumstances regard this arrangement as somehow rather indecent.' There is this sense of indecency about exposing private money to the scrutiny of others. That is why approximate income parity is a prerequisite for any degree of openness. Prurience and prudery jostle: the desire to let go, to reveal, to expose, versus a tendency to hold back, to keep covered, stay modest.

Many of us share tendencies to trivialise and to be derogatory about those who do take money seriously, and we minimise its importance: 'It's only money.' All are manifestations of this mix of prudery and prurience. Describing people's money styles, Americans Edward Hallowell and William Grace suggest money has 'psychic currency' and say: 'Most people surround their feelings about money with so much anxiety that they are unable to focus on the topic long enough and calmly enough to discover its various disguised meanings. Instead, they dismiss serious consideration with a humorous, albeit simplistic, remark like, "I wish I had more".'[15] In my own conversations with people, I found that they often used exactly this remark and would then try to slide away from the subject altogether.

Nevertheless, 'I wish I had more' signifies something more than a lighthearted way of avoiding money. It is based on envy, and envy is a powerful motivator. In *Political Passions*, Australian political psychologist the late Alan Davies wrote that 'envy begins with the breast'. He discussed the pervasive tendency to deny envy: 'What is so painful about envy? Why must we seek to hide even from ourselves this angry feeling that another possesses and enjoys something desirable and our impulse to take it away or spoil it?'[16]

The 'self-destructive and corrosive' nature of envy, combined with denial of its existence, is a potent mix when it clusters around disparities in wealth, as it often does. We may envy the actual money that people have, or envy their competence in being able to generate it. In Kleinian terms this may reflect envy of the milk, versus envy of the machinery that produces it, the breast itself. A lot of the talk about those that have money incorporates dismissal of their skill ('They were left it'; 'They were just lucky'). Envy may also be directed against one's own money; sometimes evident among the wealthy people I interviewed. It takes the form of a sort of pre-emptive denigration to ward off the envy of others. So envy may not only include envy *of* others, but also projection of our own envy *onto* others. The fear that others may envy what we have leads to secrecy, and to the need for parity before discussing personal money. A conscious or unconscious effort to ward off potentially envious attacks may lie behind not telling the children about our money — we thus protect ourselves from the child's envy.

Envy also provokes emulation, a desire to keep up with the Joneses that is fed by advertising agencies worldwide: 'With the exception of the instinct of self-preservation, the propensity for emulation is probably the strongest and most alert and persistent of the economic motives proper.'[17] Envy may underlie acquisitiveness, materialism, ambition and display. It may lead to 'spoiling' behaviour that causes people to buy something largely to prevent others having it. Envy may be visible (naked envy) but is more usually invisible. In his book

Old Money, N.W. Aldrich points out that the word envy is from the Latin *invidia*, which means, literally, 'non-sight'.[18] Denial may keep the emotion out of sight, but not out of mind, which adds to the furtiveness around money.

Embarrassment of riches

Why do people, perhaps particularly women, feel embarrassed or intimidated by riches? Though society may admire the rich, and the rich may be powerful, there is a lot that could make them feel defensive, if not completely undermined. One only needs to flick through the many anthologies of money writings or quotations to see the asperity and ridicule reserved for the wealthy. There is widespread mockery and disparagement. The following piece by the author of *Money and Class in America*, Lewis Lapham, is a particularly scathing example:

> To describe the rich as people is often to make a mistake with the language. Rich nouns or pronouns, perhaps, but not people. The rich tend to identify themselves with a sum of money, and by so doing they relinquish most of their claims to their own humanity. Their money becomes a synthetic fabrication of heart and mind, an artificial circulatory system. This is why it is so difficult to borrow from the rich, why they forget to pay their bills. To ask them for money is to ask them, literally, for blood. Having lost the capacity to distinguish between money as necessity and money as luxury and power, they imagine that the loss of the third car or the second sailboat will cause them to vanish. When preoccupied with the existential question of their net worth, the expression in their eyes narrows into a lizard's stare.[19]

In the face of that sort of withering analysis one can understand why the rich might seek to downplay their wealth. In addition, Christian teaching stresses the difficulties the rich encounter in attempting to enter the kingdom of Heaven, and Jesus memorably cast moneylenders from the temple. Centuries of injunctions by religious leaders and writers against avarice, greed, covetousness and usury have seeped into Protestant veins. This is powerfully supported in the Anglo-Celtic literary heritage, particularly in the works of Shakespeare and Dickens, creators of such characters as Shylock and Scrooge, as well as in many other novels before and since. It is not surprising that the rich may seek to make wealth seem a burden rather than a blessing. After all, it is the meek who shall inherit the earth.

Such attitudes are incorporated into the language of money. We still tend to describe someone wealthy as worth 'a small fortune' or 'a not inconsiderable fortune', reflecting this tendency to bring wealth down, to diminish it. Similarly, to describe someone as being 'of modest means' not only encapsulates the tendency to diminution: it keeps money small and demure, drawing in a notion of behavioural, even sexual, virtue.

People in upper-income groups tend to downplay their incomes so as not to appear to be outdoing peers or to be behaving ostentatiously. This self-pruning of income is possibly a peculiarly Australian trait (a kind of pre-emptive, financial tall-poppy-lopping) and perhaps, more particularly, an Anglo-Celtic Australian trait. At the time some of my interviews were taking place, two of Australia's most notable financial buccaneers of the 1980s, Alan Bond and John Elliott, were facing legal actions. Bond was an entrepreneur who began with nothing, amassed significant wealth, and lived a very public and lavish lifestyle. He, like John Elliott, retained a 'common man' image largely through backing high-profile sport along with ownership of major breweries — beer and skittles. Bond won public affection by sponsoring the successful Australian challenge to the 1983 America's Cup. He then sought to acquire cultural credentials by developing an art collection, including priceless works by Van Gogh and Matisse. His dream run was based on increasingly dubious financial foundations, however, and the whole edifice came tumbling down, leading eventually to jail for Alan Bond.

When wealth-flaunters like Bond come unstuck, the belief in financial reticence finds reinforcement. This, combined with notions of Aussie mateship and egalitarianism, ensures that wealth gets flaunted, if at all, only with some hedging. The following comments were made by two upper-income men:

'I find you often lower your income figure, depending who you're talking to. With my old school buddies I'll probably knock 30 per cent off the top to tell them. I'm too embarrassed to say I'm earning double what they are ... they'd then look at you in a different light.'

'Occasionally I find myself feeling self-conscious about what might be perceived as a display of affluence. You sort of think, Damn. I wish I hadn't bought this car.'

The second speaker found a way to mention, in the group discussion in which he was participating, his ownership of an expensive car, but he retained his egalitarian credentials with a gesture of (perhaps) false financial modesty. The note of regret does not sound terribly convincing, nor was it enough to deter the purchase. Whether or not the sentiments are genuine, however, even a touch of Anglo-Celtic guilt complicates what could otherwise be simple pleasure in success and ownership. On the other hand, there is no sign of modesty when drivers of expensive imported cars add registration plates with the word MERC or BMW. Conspicuous consumption writ clear!

The wealthy women in my research confirmed the tendency to downplay wealth. They described themselves as 'having a wealth base', avoiding the adjectives 'wealthy' or 'rich'. Banks have adopted the expression 'individuals of high net worth' to describe their wealthy customers, and we all say 'well-off', whatever that means. Old money eschews ostentation, looking disdainfully at the flamboyance of new and aspirant money. For those who were born to wealth, a feature of their childhoods was an active discouragement of money-talk and any sort of conspicuous material display: **'It was considered quite improper to ever flaunt your wealth, and you never talked about money.'**

While downplaying their own wealth, these women had a less sanguine view of wealthy males in the same situation: they thought men would be more likely to double their worth if asked. This reflected the women's belief that money was an element in male competitiveness. In fact, the upper-income men who took part in the research did not vindicate this view, though the lower-income men were more likely to describe themselves as middle-income than were the lower-income women. The income level reflected in the wealthy women's groups, however, was much higher than that of the other upper-income groups. This disparity may provoke different behaviour among their wealthy male counterparts, or less wealthy acquaintances. Importantly, it reveals the sort of pressures wealthy women face in forming relationships, that men may feel obliged to compete by overstating rather than understating their worth.

In all nations, and in many periods of history, the rich provide scapegoats when things are not going well. Dr Mahathir, Prime Minister of Malaysia, found it convenient to blame wealthy American investor George Soros for Malaysia's 1998 financial troubles — accusations that could readily invoke images of usury and 'grubby' money dealings, whether true or not. Since the rich in some countries may be associated with particular racial sub-groups, it is easy for anti-rich feelings to be anti-racial feelings. One can provide an excuse for the other. In such situations one's life may depend upon hiding one's wealth.

We are quick to tell ourselves, our children and each other that wealth doesn't bring happiness, and we can usually draw on persuasive examples. But we still find it difficult to believe that the rich can feel oppressed by their wealth and, if we do, it is even more difficult to feel sympathetic. The rich suffer further in the knowledge that, no matter how miserable their upbringings, no matter how hard they work, it is difficult for them to access one major indulgence: unless they pay a therapist for a professional ear, which is not quite the same, money can't buy sympathy. It may even preclude it.

The rich are not the only ones to feel embarrassed about their level of income. People on low incomes are just as likely to prevaricate about their money. Research sometimes indicates that the poor have more in common with the rich than either group has in common with people of middle incomes. For example, both rich and poor may tend to withdraw from normal social and economic intercourse. Both groups often lack proper career experience, drifting in and out of jobs. Both may experience the awkwardness that others feel in their presence. Both poverty and richness can appear infectious. People steer away from poverty because it makes them feel bad, and after conducting interviews with the very wealthy I often walked out into the street feeling rich.

Embarrassment, financial modesty, prudery and prurience are symptoms of money's private and secret life. In the early chapters of this book we explored the conscious inheritance of money memories and experiences from childhood. We saw that these continue to have a powerful effect on our adult money attitudes and behaviours. Psychoanalytic theories go further and place money-attitude development in infancy and intimacy.

The psychoanalytic theorists charted the first steps in the outward connection of the self to others. Klein detailed the infant's discovery of its own 'otherness' and then of particular others in its environment, especially the mother. In the Freudian money scenario, the child develops a sense of autonomy, and some power over others, via exercise and control of the bowel. Since money attitudes can be connected to the infant's emerging sense of autonomy, of otherness and of control, this begins to link into the area of money and power.

Even the most persistent Scrooge has to use money externally sometimes. We do have to take our personal money baggage out from its internal space into relationships with the outside world and deal with questions of control and power.

8

Control Becomes Power

It is easy to accept that power *is* the most important aspect of money. Phrases such as 'money is power' or 'the power of money' have become so much an accepted wisdom that the nexus is taken for granted. It is in this sense that money and control are most often linked. Here money is externalised and visible; it is money made manifest, outside the confines of the personal psyche and the personal pocket or wallet. This can be observed and measured and is therefore a subject of much more research and analysis. This chapter looks at money and power in the family, tipping behaviour in restaurants, and the issue of inheriting money.

Money arrangements in households

The first point at which money comes out is usually within the family — in money relations between partners and between adults and children. The circles then extend outwards into money relations with relatives, friends, employees, employers, accountants, the taxation department and so on. Instances of money-in-action in these extending circles begin in the home with housekeeping allowances, budgets, spending priorities, banking arrangements, pocket money and inheritance. Extending beyond the domestic and into relationships with outside others may be questions about money-as-gifts, insurance, donations, gambling, tipping and the timing of bill payments. Beyond this second circle of money-power in action is a third area of government financial and social policy issues, such as welfare payments and fiscal policy.

In all instances, personal attitudes to money are revealed as they touch against other, sometimes very different, attitudes. The idiosyncratic and precarious nature of our own personal money-control patterns, as discussed in the previous chapters, helps to explain why such money exchanges can seem so difficult. We like to keep our money affairs under wraps and can be perplexed by and intolerant of others' monetary arrangements and attitudes. It helps to explain why money can be used (or perceived) in relation to others as a potent and aggressive weapon, and why money and power are so often linked.

The linkage between money and power is complex. Meredith Edwards' research in Australia and Jan Pahl's in Britain have demonstrated the household variations of money–power–control through their analyses of differing money allocation systems.[1] Carolyn Vogler with Jan Pahl described five basic systems of money management in households: wife management, husband management, the allowance system, pooling or shared management, and independent management. Both Pahl and Edwards point out the important distinction between control of money and management of money. Pahl describes the distinction in this way:

> *Control* is mainly exercised at the point where money enters the household. It is concerned with decisions such as which allocative system should be adopted within the household, which spouse should have the final say on

major financial decisions, and with the extent to which spouses have control over personal spending money of their own and access to joint money. *Management* is concerned with putting into operation the particular allocative system which the couple have adopted.

Their work illustrates that there are different types of power, differing opportunities for exercising that power, and differing levels of power. It places management of household money, for example, at a day-to-day and, perhaps, less 'important' level. Pahl describes low-income households where wives often managed the finances, which is not the same as controlling the finances. In this and other groups (even among the joint-pooling couples), inequalities in decision-making, in access to money resources, and in personal spending money, were widespread. It shows that money is not always power. It depends whose money it is, who controls it, what its source is, and what its purpose is. It depends on complex arrangements among the individuals concerned, their personal ideologies as well as broader national ideologies and cultures.

By controlling information about money, people have power over others. Within the family, this has traditionally been the father's domain, though this may be changing as more women enter the full-time workforce and joint accounts become more common. Indeed, such changes are decried by conservative thinkers (and conservative politicians) as undermining social and economic stability. For example, traditionalists argue that the 'bourgeois' family is at the core of entrepreneurialism, and forms the basis of advanced Western capitalism and its social and political forms. It is argued that the distinctive characteristics of the middle-class family revolve around the sanctity of private property, primogeniture, and marriages based on choice and self-sufficiency. These in turn, the argument goes, encourage individualism, hard work, training, parsimony and saving.[2]

The increasing incidence of joint bank accounts seems, on

the surface, to indicate increasing equality and greater power-sharing. However, Supriya Singh's Australian research demonstrated the ideological complexities at work when she looked into the joint account. She interpreted the joint account as 'a secular ritual' and described the way in which its 'jointness' often served to mask the continuing inequality within marriages.

Singh also points out that technology is changing the power–control–management picture of money in marriages. For example, detailed credit-card statements and readily accessible account balances mean that the money manager (who is often female) has access to a lot more information than may have been the case in the past. On the other hand, increasingly technical banking and personal financial-management systems (computer software packages) may again tend towards men controlling the information about money in marriage.[3]

In the 1930s, psychoanalyst Otto Fenichel argued that the commandeering of financial matters by males, and by the controlling classes over other classes of society, was a means of deliberately keeping the masses in ignorance and thus exercising power. He suggested there was a reciprocity between instincts and a social system which reinforced those instincts: 'The will to power on the one hand and the will to possession on the other, are roots of the desire to amass wealth. They … are most intimately intertwined.'[4] He saw this power drive as beginning in the family, around patriarchal systems, and extending from there into the social fabric:

> The fact that in the family circle money matters (like sexual matters) are reserved for the father, who maintains his domination over wife and child through their practical economic dependence on him, creates just that nimbus of 'the mysterious' which at the present time appertains to the financial field as frequently as to the sexual.

The class basis to Fenichel's analysis of money and power may seem dated, but some aspects have changed less than we imagine. More than half a century later, one wealthy person I interviewed described her early memory of money: '**There wasn't a lot of money. We didn't have holidays, all the money went into Dad's business and the main thing I remember was control. I can remember Mum always telling us how to manipulate the breadwinner to get what she wanted.**'

In more general terms, we have already discovered that, in the 1990s, money is still surrounded with secrecy, the association with sexual prudery is still there, and some of the facts haven't changed. There is continuing evidence that in low-income households wives are more likely to manage the money than husbands, and that this management does not equate with control, power, equity or equality. Pahl and Singh demonstrate the continuing force of a patriarchal ideology that sees even breadwinning wives 'holding back' the exercise of power. Despite moves towards an ideology of financial equality, often expressed through the joint account, money-power remains gendered: wives tend to manage weekly food and household/child spending, while larger items, larger financial decisions and the exercise of autonomous spending remain mostly the husbands' responsibility.

In my study, in response to the question 'Who do you think really *controls* the money in your household?', 13 per cent of women said they did, compared with 38 per cent of the male respondents claiming control. Twenty-six per cent of women said their male partner controlled the money, compared with 19 per cent of men ascribing control to the female partner. Fifty-six per cent of female respondents said they controlled household money 'equally' with partners, compared with 43 per cent of the male respondents claiming equal control.

When asked 'Who usually *manages* the money in your household?', 30 per cent of women said they did, compared with 38 per cent of men claiming management. Twenty-six per cent of women ascribed management to their husbands, while 38 per cent of men ascribed management to their wives. Forty-three per cent of women said money was jointly managed, compared with 24 per cent of the male respondents.[5]

Control continued to be a male domain, while management saw more women in the primary role. It is also important to remember that the responses illustrate perceptions, or admissions, not necessarily practices. More women, for example, claimed jointness of control or management than did men. This might mean it was a fact or it might mean that women are more inclined to espouse an ideology of jointness while men are more likely, especially in front of other men, to want to sound like the traditional male patriarch. Without interviewing both partners in the same relationship it is difficult to draw conclusions.

In 1929, Virginia Woolf suggested that all a woman needed for a sense of autonomy was '500 pounds and a room of one's own'. The 1990s feminist author Naomi Wolf, in *Fire With Fire,* discusses the difficulty she experienced in coming to terms with her increasing earning power. She says: 'lack of confidence about power and money is shared by women the world over ... It looked as though men and women of the same social class were taught two different languages about money, one that enabled and one that disabled ... it seemed as if the two genders saw themselves as inhabiting separate economies.'[6] For many women, money inhabits a world that seems 'dirty and selfish' and 'women lack a positive emotional vocabulary about money'. Naomi Wolf's growing acceptance of financial success, and the power it could confer, sounds very similar to Virginia Woolf's description, almost 70 years earlier, of the social and emotional change in her attitude brought about by having independent means. Naomi Wolf, writing in 1994, says: 'I began to see how a measure of financial autonomy had helped to burn away the invisible veil of economic fear that had shrouded me ever since I could remember ... I felt in a new way that the easing of financial fear was more fundamental to female liberation than were any of the other, more ideological and social, issues that often take priority in feminism.'

Fifty-six per cent of the women in my sample said their household money was in both joint and separate accounts, 30 per cent said it was in joint accounts only. Among the men, 62 per cent said the money was in joint accounts only, 24 per cent in both joint and separate accounts. The incidence of primarily separate accounts was on a par: 13 per cent for women, 14 per cent for men. Thus when it came to actual accounts, men look as though they have acceded to jointness (though many say that having a joint account is nothing to do with jointness, but is only a device to reduce bank fees). But when it was a matter of control, or even management, a more traditional picture remained.

In general, these numerical findings raise more questions than they answer. For example, it seems surprising that the male respondents, selected on the same criteria as the female respondents, claimed a much higher incidence of joint accounts — double that of the women. How much is fact? How much can be ascribed to 'socially acceptable' response? Are women more candid than men, or vice versa? Does a small amount of sharing feel 'bigger' to a man than to a woman? All of these questions illustrate the great complexity of money and of domestic control and management issues, particularly those surrounding the 'ideology of jointness'.[7] They indicate that much more research is needed into the intra-household economy, and that both partners in a relationship must be interviewed in order to pinpoint their individual versions of the money experience.

Young adults in the 1990s may seem more financially literate than their predecessors, information being more accessible. Also, attitudes to such things as credit may be changing.[8] Young adults today, for example, are more tolerant of debt than were their parents. As a group they may be more in debt — at the start of working lives their incomes are usually lower, many are paying off houses and have young children. And they also tend not to see credit as debt. But still, personal money remains in what Fenichel described as the 'nimbus of the mysterious' for many people. The secrecy and privacy does confer a certain powerlessness. One partner in a relationship may feel the powerlessness in relation to another; children may feel it in relation to parents; adults in relation to financial institutions, such as banks; adults and institutions in relation to government institutions or processes.

Australian social researcher Hugh Mackay observed that there is often a sense of powerlessness in relation to 'large' amounts of money.[9] Many people I interviewed commented that 'large amounts of money seem to have a life of their own'. One informant said that a board on which he serves commits itself to large items of expenditure with a kind of swashbuckling ease, but then will carp and cavil over small amounts. A sense of powerlessness in relation to large institutions such as banks leads people to assert themselves over small amounts, to strike small blows, and thereby attain some satisfaction. Mackay says: 'even paying off a Bankcard account without incurring any interest can bring more than financial satisfaction, because it symbolises the idea of "getting on top of the system" ... And when customers feel that a bank has made a significant error, they take particular pleasure in complaining because they feel that, for once, the power is on their side.'

Perhaps this gives a clue to the appeal of the St George Bank in Australia. It began as a local cooperative building society in the 1930s and became a full-service bank only in 1992. The name is an historical accident, being the name of the local area in which it has its roots. But it was a felicitous accident, especially in the light of all the territory we have explored. Consciously or unconsciously, it positions the bank on the side of the small against the large, the powerless against the powerful. St George has grown to become one of Australia's largest banks. Its challenge will be to maintain this sense of itself as a David among Goliaths.

Tipping: power and status in restaurants

A fascinating example of the exercise of money-power outside the home is in the matter of restaurant tipping. Talking to people about this subject proved to be a good way of uncovering underlying attitudes to money (and to life). Not everyone would agree with the notoriously mean J. Paul Getty, who said: 'It is rude and inconsiderate to overtip. It only makes it more difficult — and embarrassing — for people who are not as rich as I am.'

Every nation has its conventions — mostly unwritten — about tipping. Many a tired traveller has experienced the start to an overseas holiday when, hot, flustered and laden with baggage, one wrestles in mind as well as pocket to find the 'right' amount to tip a porter. Some people enjoy the power, the sense of largesse displayed in a tip. Others find the whole business undignified and discomforting. 'Tip' is allegedly an acronym, originating in eighteenth-century English pubs where coins were attached to notes to the waiter 'To Insure Promptness'. The following quotation is from a man who was very upfront in his expectations of promptness: **'If I go to a restaurant and it's really crowded and I can see there's going to be a long wait, what I do is tip upfront: "My name's Fred, what's yours? Hello Susie, here's $20. I don't want you to share it. Make sure we don't run out of drinks, just look after us." And it works really well because then you're buying good service.'**

This example shows that tipping is not only about buying or rewarding good service, nor only about impressing the recipient. When it takes place in a social setting it is as much about impressing others — impressing a partner or group, or even strangers — with the extent of one's munificence or influence. There are two questions involved in tipping: Should one tip at all? And how much should one tip? Uncertainty surrounds the precise quantity: How much *is* the 'right' amount in order to acknowledge good service without seeming too mean, on the one hand, or too showy on the other? Again it is about finding the right balance.

Men and women may judge the 'right balance' differently. One American study showed that men tipped almost twice as much as women. The study also showed that the percentage customers left in tips did not correlate with their ratings of the atmosphere, or the food, or even with their ratings of the service in the restaurant. So tipping is about something else altogether. The higher level of men's tips illustrates a connection not simply between money use and income level but also between money and status, power and competitiveness. The imbalance in the relationship between customer and waiter, the exercise of power, and social pressures involved in the semi-public nature of the tipping transaction may lead to those moments when a wife looks fed up with her husband's apparently 'uncharacteristic' generosity. Another American study found that if waiters made some sort of light, often unnoticeable, physical contact (a brief shoulder brush or a hand touch when returning change) they were left a slightly larger tip than those waiters in a control group who did not touch the customer![10]

All this suggests that tipping involves a number of complex and interconnected issues, making it a surprisingly difficult area to research. To begin with, if it is left to customers and waiters to self-report the tipped amount, both giver and receiver are likely to lie: customers want to seem more generous than they are; waiters want to seem more successful. It also tends to confirm the perception of the women in my research who felt that men use money as an extension of their egos and as a unit of competition. It certainly confirms that tipping is an example of money–power–control in action, and that money use is an extension of emotional and psychological factors.

Research into the effect of group size on tipping behaviour

is also interesting, though not yet definitive. One study showed that the bigger the group the smaller the percentage tipped. Tables of one tipped nearly twice as much as tables of four or six people. The researchers suggest that the reason lies in 'diffusion of responsibility' in the group. That is, the larger group renders the exchange less personal, more anonymous, and individuals can therefore 'hide' in group responsibility. Other research, however, suggests that the explanation is one of equity, that it is practical rather than psychological — larger groups require less effort, per person, from the waiter.[11]

There is also some research evidence that found credit-card payers give larger tips than cash payers.[12] This seems a bit surprising since cash has been shown to feel more personal than cards. Gender factors may be at work here, however; card payers may have been male rather than female, and men tip more than women. It is also possible that cash, precisely because it is more personal, may feel like a more significant gift, even if the amount is smaller, than does merely adding a digit to a credit-card slip. Anonymity was a factor in the question of group size, and it is a central question in the matter of card versus cash tipping. However, the issue was complicated by the fact that payment by card took place at a more expensive restaurant where service levels were higher. It did not find the expected inverse connection between tip size and group size because the customers did not feel like anonymous members of a group. These are very interesting areas, requiring research that holds variables such as restaurant type (expensive or cheap), gender and group size more constant than has been the case thus far.

In my own research, I found that most people, of both genders and in all income groups, felt uncomfortable and ambivalent about tipping. In *Profile of Australia*, writer Craig McGregor said: 'Australians sit beside the taxi driver on the front seat, drift easily between public and saloon bar in the pub, dislike tipping because it implies a servile relationship ... arrogance is the worst sin and deference the next.'[13] Egalitarianism, combined with a general discomfort about money, adds up to an awkwardness about tipping that was elaborately rationalised by people in my discussions — often by making comparisons with overseas practices. Those who do not tip waiters excused themselves, claiming that waiters are paid enough here, unlike waiters in the United States, who depend on tips. Some said they would only tip if the service were extraordinarily good. Most just rounded up the bill to an amount a little above the total, adding the tip on to whatever form of payment it suited them to use on that occasion, credit card or cash.

A vocal minority, however, always tried to tip in cash because 'then it goes to the person' or 'it seems more personal'. As well as demonstrating a lingering association of cash with humanness, and cash with food, this is also an exercise in trying to keep control over the money, keeping a personal connection with the transaction rather than have it disappear into an amorphous and impersonal slush fund.

American social anthropologist Viviana Zelizer says tipping lies 'at the boundary of other critically different transfers, not quite a payment, not quite a bribe, not quite charity, but not quite a gift either ... tips indicated distance and inequality between donor and recipient'.[14] It is this very inequality that gives some tippers a sense of power but leaves others feeling uncomfortable. Zelizer maintains that the move to make tips a part of wage entitlement, not a gift, in the United States has helped to overcome the discomfort. The parents in my research who give pocket money as an entitlement are presumably seeking to avoid a similar discomfort. Dispensing pocket money to children, or tips to waiters, is an exercise in money power and control, enjoyable for some, uncomfortable for others, and involving all that is complex about money and relationships. In both instances, money can be seen operating in its role as a medium of symbolic, psychosocial exchange as much as it is a medium of material exchange.

One of the issues linking discomfort about money-gifts, tipping and discomfort about money-talk in general is parity. A disparity of income, status and power is potentially exposed in these transactions. Money-talk is only comfortable, as we have observed, when there is a level of income equivalence or parity. Gift-giving is a tricky business because it involves efforts to maintain some sort of equivalence in the exchanges. Out-of-balance gifts can be embarrassing for the recipient but even for the donor who has 'misjudged' the balance. Sociologists talk about the norm of reciprocity that ensures ongoing harmony in social interaction. David Cheal's study of gift-giving in Canada describes gifts as 'symbolic media for managing the emotional aspects of relationships'.[15] Sometimes it is acceptable for there to be asymmetry (when there are status differences, such as between an adult and a child, or boss and employee) but usually people aim for some symmetry. When gifts consist of objects, then precise value is harder to know, and therefore apparent symmetry or equivalence is easier to achieve. When gifts of money are involved, however, then nothing is left to the imagination, allowing crass-seeming asymmetries to occur. Ritualised money gift-giving, such as wedding money or even funeral money, may be different and has its own cultural 'rules'. But the Anglo-Celt looks a bit askance at such practices, despite their evident practicality. Or perhaps because of their practicality.

Tipping is an asymmetrical transaction. For some people this makes it easy, because economic status and responsibility are, for that moment, clearly on one side. The awkwardness comes for those used to egalitarian patterns of reciprocity, who feel obliged to respond in a hierarchical, or patronising, manner. Being on the receiving end may be no less awkward. As with most of our money behaviour, tipping is a matter of fine balance.

Pennies from heaven: power and inheritance

The more money there is, the more nakedly are power and control issues exposed. This is especially true where inherited wealth is involved. Inheritance, or even the prospect of inheritance, is often used, explicitly or implicitly, to exert control over family members. Wills and trusts may be wielded to extend that control even beyond the grave. American sociologist Marcia Millman says: 'Even if money can't shield us from death, it can buy a certain kind of immortality. Some old people comfort themselves by thinking of how they can control future generations by the way they arrange their legacies.'[16] According to a recent newspaper article, wealthy Australian industrialist Lang Hancock, for example, tried to include in his will the requirement that any beneficiary who questioned the will could not inherit.

When I asked wealthy people for their early money memories, they frequently responded with variations of 'my grandfather used money to control us'; 'my father was into control'. For many of them, power, control, love and money seemed inextricably connected. This had led to some painstaking, and painful, efforts to disentangle the connections:

'I was always equating his love for me with his power and money. From my point of view, he used his money unethically. I mean as well as being a loving, cuddly grandfather he was also a prick. So I connected all that together and I thought, I don't want that money–power–love package, I don't want the whole thing. So then I couldn't have the money, or power, or love. I didn't care about the money or the power, but I had to sort of pick them apart, to take them separately, not to lock them all in.'

For someone who inherits wealth, or is part of a wealthy family, the first 'external' manifestation of power and control is that exerted upon them by an older generation. The second is the power that having money might give them. The wealthy women in my research recognised that their wealth did indeed give them power. They defined this power as freedom, choice, autonomy and access to influential networks: **'You have the power to do what you want to. You develop great competencies, a sense of your own empowerment. And that's tremendously threatening in a woman when it's backed up with knowledge, with contacts, with money. Because with money comes the ability to get all of these things and that's as threatening as the actual cash itself. I think the use of the word 'money' worries me. I see wealth, I see influence, I see power. I mean you can live in a place that's worth a million dollars and have $100 income, but you've still got the power of knowing that you can mortgage that place, you can do things. And the contacts. Even if you are the really poor part of a wealthy family, you've got power.'**

A third aspect of this power and control is the way the wealth affects others. Closest to home there is the question of what to say about money to one's own children. The wealthy people I talked to were trying to carve a pathway for their children which acknowledged the money but pointed out that self-esteem would only be served by children making their own way, almost despite the wealth. They described money as 'the landing pad' or the 'armchair', but were concerned to convey that it was not a substitute for personal enterprise. In all income groups, parents worry about their children taking money for granted. For the wealthy, however, there is a more pressing fear of the potentially undermining, enervating power of wealth. Wealthy parents placed less emphasis on the mechanics of daily money life and the exhortations to save that were the hallmark of financial instruction in other income groups. Large wealth created different priorities, based around self-esteem, independence, careers, and not taking wealth for granted. For those who have inherited wealth, concern about children's dependency is a projection of their own struggles to build an independent sense of self-worth.

It was interesting to listen to wealthy women discussing whether and how to tell children about their money. Both the terminology and the tone of these discussions sounded very similar to telling children about sex, with such comments as 'They can only handle a little at a time' and 'It's too much to take in at once'.

'My son came home from school one day and he said, "Mum, are we rich?" I thought, Oh goodness, it's THE question! And I was sort of gearing up for the big deep and meaningful. To delay it I said, "Why do you ask?" He replied, "Because this kid stopped me on the way home from school and he said you've got good clothes, you must be rich." My son was in a school jumper and clean jeans that day! So I'm using that to illustrate the point that there are so many cues that constantly need processing ... I think it's one of the strains of being wealthy, that one has to adjust the focus in all sorts of ways, many of which are subtle.'

It illustrates a more general difficulty we all have in explaining money to our children. As we have already discovered, most of us keep our money attitudes private, even from ourselves. Our thinking, if we do it at all, is often primitive and irrational. It is not easy in these circumstances to sound like a competent, mature adult in the face of children's questions. As with sex questions, euphemisms and evasions abound. On top of that there is the complication, evident at all income levels, of context and of relativity. What is 'wealth'? Even if we accept a narrow pecuniary definition, we are rich in some contexts, poor in others.

There is no doubt that being both wealthy and female adds another complex layer to the money–power question. Some people tacitly agree with the aphorism 'Nothing is more intolerable than a wealthy woman'.[17] Though men (and women) may protest that they would be untroubled by an imbalance, there is plenty of evidence that when the female in a relationship is richer than the male, whether based on earnings or inheritance, there are problems for both parties. The women that I interviewed said their wealth often created difficulties in their personal relationships, difficulties based upon inequality of status or power: '**I have never, ever known even as a friend any man who has got anywhere near as much money as I have. The men I have known as friends and lovers have generally been of modest means, so it's always been an issue in relationships. There's tension, there's envy, there's self-consciousness. There's a sort of fantasy that things would be better if only we were more equal in terms of assets.**'

Talking about personal money is a delicate business. At all income levels it requires a certain parity of income before people can begin to feel comfortable. All the more reason, therefore, that wealthy women experience major difficulty in relationships where large income disparity is often involved. Conventional gender roles and power balances are topsy-turvy, for both parties. Although the women recognised that male partners made contributions in other ways: 'When it comes to handing over the cheque for the shopping, it's still really difficult. It's difficult for him and difficult for me!' There was sometimes a confusing, but inescapable, hankering for dependency: 'I have to confess that basically I want the man to take care of me but, on the other hand, I've got more money than him.' American psychiatrist Sheila Klebanow identifies this as basically a fear of abandonment.

Many of the women I talked to had grown up in families where they were regarded as less competent than their brothers. Their fathers had tended not to 'educate' them about the family businesses or family money. They often lacked confidence and competence, not only about money. They resisted the possibility that they may be using their money to control others in the same way as had their parents, particularly fathers. Several had joined a philanthropic network for wealthy women, indicating an active desire to use wealth differently from their fathers, and to allay guilt about their fortunate financial positions.

Because a large part of their current wealth was inherited, it felt 'unearned' and was often treated differently from money they had made or earned themselves. These findings confirm the view of social anthropologists such as Belk and Wallendorf and Zelizer that money is not undifferentiated, homogeneous, or unitary.[18] Different sources of money make money 'feel' different, and money may be used in different ways, depending on that source. One of the younger women described it in this way: **'I enjoy the money I make more than the money I'm given. I'm so much happier to spend it. But with the money I'm given I don't want to blow it and I don't want to rely on it, so I just invest it and leave it alone. I don't feel bad about spending the money I make because I know how hard I worked to get it and I know I can do it again.'**

A 'hands-off' approach to inheritance — leave it alone or give it away — may not be typical of the wealthy in general. The wealthy often feel a particular obligation to inherited money, a duty to keep it going. In his book *The Money Motive,* Thomas Wiseman describes inherited money as 'like royal descent, carrying with it powerful coercive elements'. Inheritors have a 'sense of obligation *to the money*, as if it were living stuff ...'

> It is endowed with a life of its own. People talk of Krupp money, or Ford money, or Guinness money, as if the family genes are somehow incorporated in it. To preserve it, and multiply it, is to transmit the strain, keep the stock *viable*. Blood may be thicker than water, but money is thicker than both.[19]

The money-as-blood metaphor calls to mind both Hobbes and Marx, quoted in the earlier chapter on economics and money. In 1996 in Australia, the Myer and Coles families felt impelled to involve themselves in boardroom upheavals in the huge Coles Myer retail empire. The third generation, including members of the family not directly involved in the running of the businesses, spoke out. When the stocks (metaphorically and literally) were down, family members rallied on behalf of the financial bloodline. This was not only to protect their income source, but also to protect the family name and reputation, something like the 'incorporated family genes' that Wiseman describes.

Inheritance is a complex matter, even when the amounts involved are small. One person I spoke to in the lower-income category referred to the terrible awkwardness of being left money by a relative while her siblings missed out. Ironically, she invested the money in a building society that collapsed and she lost the lot. There are many similar stories of inheritances being lost or squandered, as if unconsciously to undo the gift. Certainly this woman said that in some ways she felt better for having lost the money, relieved of the burden of gratitude and the barbs of envy. A man expressed another sort of ambivalence: **'It was a terrific thing, to get that cash injection. It's not that you want it — you'd rather have your parents here — but I had mixed feelings. The cash was a great help but you think, Why on earth didn't they do something with it? Why have I got it?'**

Today's parents, of whatever income level, believe in enjoying themselves now rather than putting their money away for a rainy day, as many of their own parents had done before. This means that, though keen to give their children some financial assistance, they are not prepared to sacrifice too much: **'It used to bug me when my parents said, "We're leaving it for you". I used to say to Mum, "Go and spend it, enjoy it". I certainly don't feel like that for my children; they've got to make their own way in this life. There'll probably be something left for them but they shouldn't expect it.'**

Writing about the American middle-class, Marcia Millman says: 'For most of this century, the primary legacy of middle-class parents to children has been "cultural capital" — the upbringing and education that allowed children to become financially successful and independent of their parents'.[20] To give one's children 'a good start in life' was the main goal of most of the parents I interviewed. While bemoaning the huge outlay on private school fees and orthodontic bills, one mother said: '**I tell my children they're getting a good education and good teeth!**'

Parents believe that this larger lesson in deferring gratification is in children's best interests. They hope to teach their children that they will have to earn their own money rather than rely on an 'instant' or automatic source. There are to be no illusions of omnipotence or inexhaustible supply. Nevertheless, children will usually stand to inherit assets such as houses, possessions, shares and so on. Millman points out that the generation of parents now in their fifties to seventies have amassed considerable assets that will pass mostly to their offspring. It is estimated that in the United States alone this will amount to a $US7–8 trillion transfer of wealth in the next twenty years. Modifying this picture somewhat is the likelihood that children will remain dependent well into young adult life, as they complete further educational qualifications and/or find themselves unemployed, or financially strapped after divorces.

Inheritance is unlike other forms of windfall money (such as lottery winnings) in that it rests on another's efforts. As Winston Churchill put it: 'Saving is a very fine thing. Especially when your parents have done it for you.' The emotional strings that are attached to inheritance often cause feelings of guilt. One woman said: '**I really struggle to spend money on myself. I'm sure it's tied up with self-esteem and that I didn't earn it. We just happened to be there; our parents made it.**'

The 'bag lady' syndrome describes wealthy people who go to great lengths to hide their wealth, living and dressing dowdily in order not to draw attention, to avoid being set apart. Whether consciously or not, this may also be a way to avoid being 'put upon' by others, or it may even mask chronic miserliness. Wealthy American philanthropist Tracy Gary tells the story of an heiress who wanted to escape all the potential problems she thought would be associated with inheriting great wealth. With enormous effort and difficulty, she relinquished her inheritance and moved to the other end of the country. She took up work as a jobbing gardener and spent many years in this way, anonymously and happily. But one of her clients died and unexpectedly left her five million dollars.

As discussed in a previous chapter, many of those I interviewed who grew up in high-income families were explicitly instructed by parents never to flaunt their wealth. One said: '**Yes, it was sort of embarrassing because at school you couldn't let anyone else know anything. I think my parents were embarrassed by our wealth, and we were, too. We totally acted like pigs to make sure no-one thought we were up ourselves.**' And from another: '**When I was fifteen I got myself a job in the holidays which my father was really angry about. But it felt so good. I had a rotten childhood, but I didn't earn the money I inherited. It's taken me years to come to grips with it.**' The father, in this case, was presumably angry about losing power and control over his daughter. The daughter is still, in her late-forties, struggling to free herself from that very control (even after his death), as well as from her own guilt.

Another reaction some people have to the prospect of inheritance can be a driving need to establish self-control, to prove they can either live without money or that they can make it themselves. This is a push for autonomy, an attempt to shrug off the controlling money-power of parents. It may lead to refusing financial support from parents for university study, or travelling overseas on a shoestring: '**Proving I could live and work in my own way was an accomplishment, and once I'd done that I could feel now I'll have the money!**'

The controlling power of money is much more apparent when wealth is involved. Arguments over inheritance in rich families are notorious and often public (though probably no less frequent in poorer families or where small amounts of money are involved). A struggle for control was apparent in all income groups in my research, but more explicitly so for the wealthy. Some of the wealthy women I interviewed had met through a common interest in being what they called 'active donors'. The psychological benefit of taking their money by the ears, as it were, and using it constructively reflected their need to take control over money, rather than have the money control them. The whole area of inheritance illustrates again that money-source does influence money-attitude and money-usage, and that people do make such differentiations. There was a feeling that a large amount of money can be somehow dangerous, volatile, with a life of its own. Inheritance was sometimes a poisoned chalice to be handled with extreme care. Beneficiaries could try to run away from their inheritance, try to share it, try to protect it, try to spend it, or save it, or give it away. One way or another, however, they finally had to come to terms with it, to tame it.

Fear of success is another possible outcome of living in the shadow of wealth. In the words of one wealthy woman: '**I've rebelled the other way. There was no way I was going to become independent. I suppose there was a big fear of success because if I went into any form of business or made any form of money then I would have to do what my father did and be totally driven. I had no interest in that whatsoever.**' This sense that there was no other way but to follow the father, to be 'driven', reflects a marked lack of autonomy and a fear of the perceived connection between money and power. Fear of success is a complex, multi-layered phenomenon, sometimes involving family relationships, sometimes playing itself out in neurotic, self-defeating financial behaviour as described by Edmund Bergler in an earlier chapter.

There is also a broader cultural layer involved in societies where success (particularly wealth) breeds resentment and scepticism rather than praise. This so-called 'tall poppy syndrome' is evident in Australia. In his book *Fear of Success*, David Tresemer suggests that 'Society is very much engaged in the moral training of the individual to avoid narcissistic success'.[21] Tresemer discusses the 'turning wheel of fate' that leads people to anticipate, or fear, the inevitable downside of success. 'Belittling oneself, hiding or explaining away successes, persistent concentration on negative possibilities — these are as amulets to ward off the danger imminent to the successful and to start the wheel back on its upward course.'

Fear of success may be of particular significance for women, especially where money is concerned. Research generally shows that women will tend to undervalue themselves, literally, in the marketplace, and in couples where the woman earns more than the man, there are problems for both parties. Reporting on the study of 20 000 *Psychology Today* readers, American researcher Carin Rubenstein said:

> Some women seem intimidated by their unexpectedly large earning power. A 33-year-old San Franciscan admitted that she was 'scared to death' when she realised that, through sales commissions, she could earn as much as she wanted. She stopped working in June, having already earned $30,000 in six months, with endless questions about having 'too much' money: 'How to keep men from being threatened by my earning power; how to keep friends with less money and how to cope with their jealousy; how to keep from feeling guilty about the "haves" and "have nots"; how to cope with inevitable changes in my goals and values.' [Rubenstein adds] Most men do not have these problems, and those who do are rarely so candid about or so intimidated by them.[22]

This leads us to wonder whether men and women are different in their attitudes to money? Does money itself seem male? Is money sexy? These are some of the questions raised in the next chapter.

9

Money, Gender and Sex

In an American publication called *Robin Hood Was Right,* a wealthy woman says:

> Money gives you the status of a man, because money is power. Power is the name. My last name is a man's name. My name isn't forgotten in the wash. It's a special name, but all the names associated with wealth are man's names. So if women have them, people feel they're a man, effectively, in terms of power.[1]

Money has been associated traditionally with power and, hence, with maleness in Protestant, Anglo-Celtic societies. Psychoanalyst Sheila Klebanow says:

> Insofar as men made the money, men held the power. Part of the male persona, the sense of autonomy stemming from the ability to earn a living involves the perception of oneself as a power source. Perhaps in this sense men may have less neurotic conflict than women about the equation: money = power.

She describes a well-paid, successful female patient who, no matter what recognition she received for her work, no matter what salary she brought home, found it 'unfeminine' to grasp the uses of money.[2] Klebanow expresses the hope that the issue of money and male power may be transitional and concludes her chapter:

> As the next generation of women works in increasingly responsible careers, more women will learn something that perhaps some men understand better: that money is power, that it is neither "feminine" nor "masculine" to seek to be one's own effective power source but merely human.

Is money male, and is it sexy?

I tried to find out in my research groups whether the word 'money' conjures up maleness. I gave people six words to place on a continuum with 'masculine' at one end and 'feminine' at the other. The order in which the words were given, and in which the scale was presented, were varied to discourage any order bias. In order of most 'masculine-ness', the results were: investment, income, wealth, money, saving, spending. Both genders and all income groups placed the six items in the same order. The findings echo the stereotypes, with 'investment' at the masculine end of the scale and 'spending' at the feminine end: men holding it in, women letting it out. The word 'money' was placed androgynously in the middle.

A word count of all my interview transcripts revealed that, in total, fathers featured in money-talk and money-memories of both men and women and at all income levels, slightly more than mothers. Nevertheless, the role of mothers in childhood money-memory is strong because they were usually the day-to-day presence. Mothers were often the dispensers of pocket money, small money and domestic money, while fathers dealt with major expenditure and financial decisions. To that extent, 'money' in the abstract may be associated with maleness. The whole question of 'money' and its perceived gender needs to be explored without the 'clutter' of early memories and perhaps without the other items that I had included in my masculine–feminine scale. It would also be interesting to explore the perceived gender of coins versus notes, and of cash versus cards.

In Lacanian psychoanalysis 'the law of the father' is a symbolic idea signifying the person to whom we are indebted. Maturity means we are able to acknowledge the debt to this figure without feeling overwhelmed or constrained by it.[3] Maturity is also to do with becoming an effective agent of 'debt' in our own right, capable of negotiating and reciprocating. Money is one arena where we work all this out, where we develop a sense of ourselves, both morally and materially. We have explored this process in relation to pocket money: something so apparently small and innocent was seen to be a touchstone for significant issues of autonomy and individuality.

There is plenty of evidence that the equation 'money equals power' tends to be associated with maleness. Power and status issues were volunteered in my interviews with men, but very rarely from women. When power aspects of money were raised by women it was usually to ascribe it to men, and explicitly not to women: '**Men see money as a status thing.**' One man described money as '**a power commodity**'; another said, '**The measure of your worth tends to be how much you earn**'; and another, '**You gain an impression of where you stand vis-a-vis the people you mix with**'. Men talked about '**feeling empowered**' by money, giving examples such as successful bidding at auction: '**There's nothing better than buying something and knowing you've done well.**'

Property auctions are a fascinating example of money, power, and potency in action. To bid at auction, especially for something as major in personal expenditure as a house, is a particularly public display; competitiveness, bluff, success and failure are laid out for all to witness. A house auction is a form of licensed voyeurism — to look over a person's house is to look over their lives. As the auction takes place, there is a range of human emotion on view, even among those looking studiedly nonchalant. For the successful bidder there is the 'rush', the excitement, relief and perhaps some trepidation; there is the vulnerability of vendors, the transparency of their lifestyle, tastes and financial aspirations; there is the disappointment of losing bidders who had already imagined themselves into a new house, a new life. All this in the hands, for a few brief minutes, of auctioneers and agents whose role it is to encourage people to jettison their customary control and privacy.

A friend attended an auction recently, intending to buy the house as an investment property. She was an experienced investor, had done all her homework and had funds available. While waiting for the auction to start, an old school friend spied her in the crowd and came over to chat. My friend found this so inhibiting that she didn't make a single bid. The house was sold for less than she would have paid. The presence of this old acquaintance had made revealing her financial hand too personal and too public. She was astonished by her own inhibition. Others might have been encouraged to exceed their limit in similar circumstances, the situation fostering greater competitiveness. Indeed, auctions are predicated on the assumption that this is how most people respond. There is similar variation for those who just look on. Some thrill at the vicarious experience, while others cringe a bit at the explicitness of it all, the feeling that they are witnessing something so significant for the main players that it ought to remain private. As with anything 'gladiatorial', the spectacle and the spectators can be both compelling and repugnant.

Research findings tend to show that for men, money is power whereas women relate to money in different ways, connected with personal and social relationships. My own findings, as discussed in the childhood memories chapter, found a similar pattern in the stories told by women: their money stories were inextricably linked to accounts of relationships. Money could barely be discussed except in this social context.

Women have been found to be more 'other-oriented' in relation to all their possessions, including money.[4]

Carol Gilligan's work compared girls and boys at play and charted their social and moral development. She asserts that female cognitive, social and moral development is found in, and based upon, connectedness, relationships and attachment.[5] In the playgound, little girls would sacrifice a game rather than have it lead to disharmony. By contrast, males learn and develop through a sense of separateness, and of hierarchy. Little boys want a clear winner and a loser. My exploration of money has, almost inadvertently, picked up and illustrated this difference in gender attitude, demonstrating how effectively money can illuminate important underlying psychosocial constructs.

Returning to the question of money, power and maleness, it was evident that men, especially in middle- and lower-income groups, were as likely to talk about powerlessness as about power. When asked what feeling or emotion they had associated with money in the past week, one man volunteered: **'Feeling powerless actually. You can have a career or job or save some money or invest some money and then some international thing happens and the value of your dollars falls through the floor and you're not responsible, you're powerless.'** This lack of control, and the impact of factors outside one's own control, could seem daunting and disheartening.

There was sometimes a rather wistful hankering for the ability to have more power, to be more in control: '**I don't feel totally powerless, but I have a vague feeling I suppose that I should learn more about money, how to take control in the future.**' This man went on to say that his father had drummed into him that '**you're ultimately responsible for your own position in life**', thus providing an example of a link between childhood maxims, male influence and current money attitudes.

Among the wealthy women, fathers were the dominant

figure in money memories, reinforcing an association of money, power and maleness. These women had a multiplicity of issues to deal with: they had often felt undervalued by their fathers, especially in financial and business affairs, compared with male siblings; they were unaccustomed to power; and they were trying to adjust to their wealth in a society where independent women may still encounter all sorts of difficulties in both personal and commercial relationships. The connection of money with power and masculinity was particularly evident in these women's experiences: **'I find it totally fascinating, having four daughters who are wealthy, how men appear to be emasculated — and it's their word as much as mine — by the woman having more money.'** And from a younger woman: **'I think they are very rare these men who are so sure of the essence of their masculinity to be at ease living with a woman of wealth and for it not to impact on their ego.'**

Some people say that money is 'sexy'. In one wealthy woman's story there emerged an association of money with potency and an important distinction made between *having* money and *making* money. The potency was clearly attached to the latter and, in this case, to the mother: **'My father was lousy rich but he didn't have any power, he didn't use the money. He put it in a sock, or a bank, or bought shares, or thought about it and wouldn't spend. Whereas mother made all the money, she turned it over all the time.'**

In that story, money is being associated with stereotypical masculinity and power (though in the quote it is the mother who 'wears the trousers'). In her book *Warm Hearts and Cold Cash*, Marcia Millman says: 'money stands behind much of what we assume to be masculinity.' She describes instances of women who out-earn their spouses and who use money to control in a way more usually associated with men. She suggests that 'a lot of what we define as "masculine" or "feminine" is actually behavior that more precisely stems from being financially dominant or dependent'.[6]

The fact remains, however, that for various socio-economic-historical-cultural reasons, men are more likely to be the financially dominant partner in a relationship. An association between money and masculinity prevails. Millman found that women are usually less likely than men to use money for control. The continuing discomfort experienced by wealthy women, or those who earn more than their male partners, was evident in my findings and has been widely noted by others.[7]

Naomi Wolf, discussing women's ambivalence about money, says: 'Women are not just ambivalent about their own money. They are ambivalent about other women's ... "Loose" female money is as threatening to the status quo as "loose" female sexuality.'[8] Thomas Wiseman notes the 'obvious sexual symbolism' of spending, claiming that extravagance equates with sexual potency and 'the man who throws his money about with élan creates a giving image of himself that women find peculiarly suggestive'. He also notes its opposite: 'The peculiarly erotic effect of spending money on a girl is emphasised by its converse: meanness is sexual anathema.'[9]

It's an interesting point, but I doubt that all women find lavish spending erotic. There is an important distinction between generosity, which is attractive, and extravagance, which may seem foolish. Lavish spending may be embarrassing for the recipient and might suggest a lack of confidence, rather than sexual élan, on the part of the spender. But in general, generosity is more desirable than meanness, and a spender may be more erotic than a saver. Meanness may well be a sexual turn-off and even its more acceptable cousin, thrift, isn't very sexy. Saving brings its own rewards though and not just financial ones, if we accept the psychoanalytic notion of anal-erotic pleasure in retention. Certainly, spending is more sociable: it can create a shared or public pleasure, while it is harder to share the pleasures of hoarding.

Bisexual and borderline money

Emerging from the research findings, and the psychoanalytic contribution, is a picture of the duality of money's gender. On the one hand it can be symbolised by the breast, by milk and motherhood — essences of femininity; on the other it is symbolised by potency and power — essences of traditional masculinity. What is clear is that money can be both of these, that it is not singular. Money is 'bisexual', varying at different times, in different circumstances. Perhaps this is why it tended to be rated in the questionnaires as gender-neutral. Official, market money, the money of banks, shares and investments, may be construed as masculine. As we saw in the previous section, potency is attached not just to a quantity of money but to the activity, the application, to the 'cut and thrust' of money.

This is the operating territory for market-money which has a language all of its own. Official money talk is, perhaps deliberately, difficult for many people to comprehend. Inscrutability keeps it in the ambit of the few: 'It doesn't sound like *my* money.' Hence the triumphant note, the sense of uncovering a secret, in the voices of the few people I interviewed who felt they had found a key to this world when they decided the national current account may be just like a household budget, writ large.

By contrast, personal money, the money of food, children and nurture, is likely to be feminine. As sociologist Supriya Singh puts it: 'It is as if money changes gender when it moves into the household.'[10] Household money is the major part of childhood money, as well as the major component of everyday money. Both in people's early memories and in the everyday use of money, cash and food go together. Cash is an important component of this domestic money, which is more feminine, and it is the area that will be involved in transitions to stored value cards.

The following diagram of a money-gender tree shows the

aspects of money that are impersonal, and largely male, and those that are personal, and largely female. The crossover points are manned (and they are usually men) by those who have to translate between the two domains, to act as interpreters when the impersonal meets the personal.

Money-gender tree

Where impersonal money meets personal, everyday money

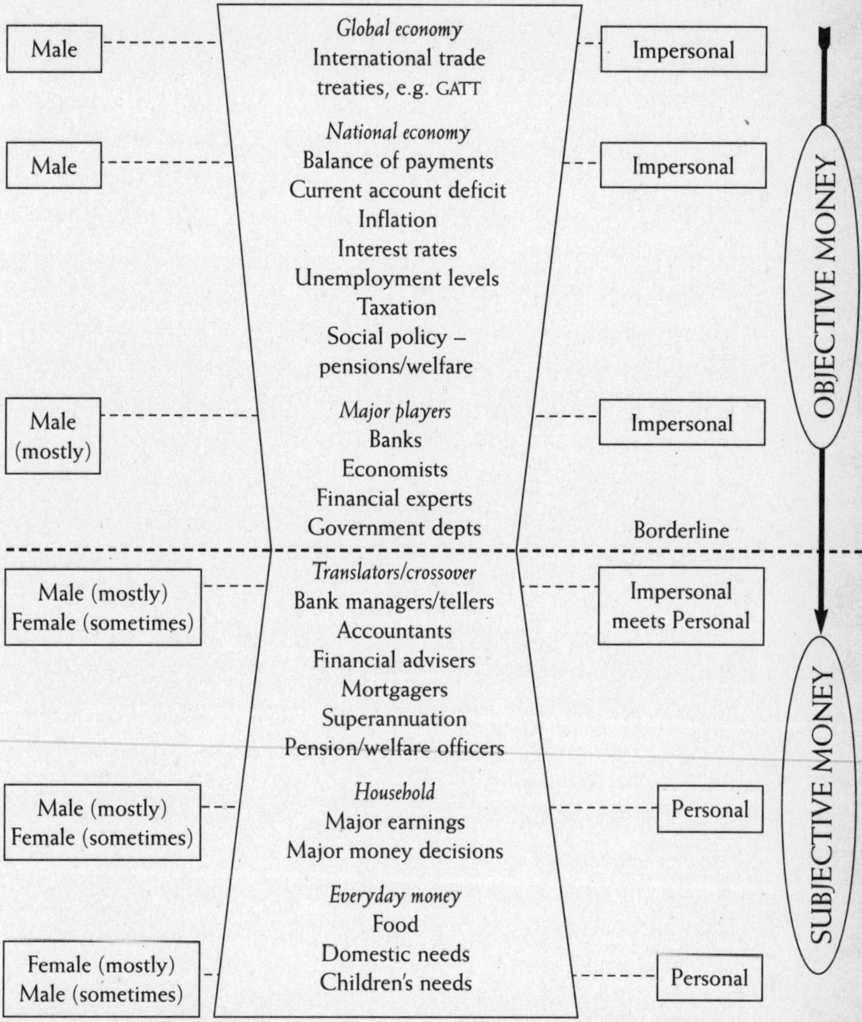

It is relatively easy to characterise two extremes of money-life as male/female or impersonal/personal. The interesting area is the territory between the two. When money has a foot in both camps, when the discourse of impersonal money meets the discourse of personal, everyday money, it is then that tensions emerge. Such tensions are due not only to the differences between those discourses but also to lack of acknowledgement of the psychosocial complexities of personal money. In other words, it is not simply a matter of the language of the two sectors being different — though people tend to blame themselves for not understanding the terminology or the concepts of 'official' money. The pressure from the predominant 'objective', economic or official discourse weighs heavily. It is constantly encroaching on the 'subjective' personal realm. Privatisation can feel like this, as can changes to superannuation policy, or asset tests: people are forced to make decisions and engage with official marketplace money in areas where they are unaccustomed and feel inadequate. Similar feelings are experienced at tax time, or when seeking a loan, as personal money is obliged to deal with impersonal, official money.

The obverse occurs when impersonal-medium-of-exchange money blunders into personal teritory. There are dramatic examples connected with birth (surrogacy payments) and death (hired killers). Children's pocket money also lies in this borderline territory because commercial (impersonal) values enter domestic (personal) territory. Gifts of money are another example, raising delicate issues about relative status and intimacy.[11] In such instances, we have to reveal our hand and it can be hard to strike the right balance because no-one talks about money. We have very few landmarks for these excursions.

Each side of the money border speaks a different language, each approaches the other with a certain incomprehension (as well as apprehension). The personal side of the border is secretive, based on a precarious sense of control and cloaked in moralism. All this combines to explain the capacity of money to provoke shock: when someone less inhibited asks how much something cost; when you hear that a friend gives her child money for getting good grades; or when someone negotiates fees with the orthodontist. The outrage that one sometimes hears in response to these border transgressions has a querulousness about it that exposes the uncertainty of the ground beneath. Partly it's envy: Why can't I be more like that? In all of this, money demonstrates its capacity to be provocative, a capacity which locates it beside other intimate areas of life.

In his now classic work *The Gift Relationship*, comparing American and British systems of blood collection, R.M. Titmuss explored the question of social altruism and payment for blood donations.[12] More recently, issues such as money changing hands for organ donations, or for surrogate pregnancy, raise questions to do with impersonal money entering territory that is deeply personal. Even the matter of amateurism versus professionalism in sport can raise passions that reveal it's not all to do with the money. Turning professional carries a faint whiff of betrayal for those legions who do it for love. Public haggling over salaries can tarnish the reputations of sporting icons. Nuns using money in the university cafeteria sometimes seemed odd to the lay onlooker, the mundanity of money and meat pies slightly undermining the sacredness of their calling! Therapists constantly have to deal with patients who feel angry about being charged for missed appointments. Care-giving, like motherhood, is not expected to be on a time-charge meter even though, rationally, clients know it has to be. As we have noted, physicians use secretaries or receptionists to mediate money, to keep the healing and the money separate. Most people, in their daily money lives, have to tread delicately across the terrain, without recourse to money mediators or shields.

The fragility of feelings at the border has to do with our money being both personal and secret. It remains fragile in the absence of advocacy: the personal experience of money has not been understood, much less publicly articulated. When we have to visit accountants at tax time, apply for bank loans or government benefits, we can feel vulnerable. When our money gets scrutinised we feel exposed because it is so personal. Linked to this sense of exposure is a sense of potential shame. In psychoanalytic terms, shame is the opposite of a sense of control, of autonomy. We blush inside at what we assume are judgements being made about our competency. We can feel stripped bare and reduced to a childlike immaturity, and there is more about this in the final chapter.

Before returning to this forbidden money territory, we will explore some practical implications of the lack of congruence between money's two faces — between its official, market face and its unofficial, personal face. By acknowledging the differences, it may be possible to effect some reconciliation of financial balance sheets with emotional balance sheets.

10

Balancing the Books: Personal and Impersonal Currency

Money is probably the most emotionally meaningful object in contemporary life; only food and sex are its close competitors as common carriers of such strong and diverse feelings, significances, and strivings.[1]

This is the context that financial institutions, indeed anyone dealing with people and money, need to understand. It is complicated, but grasping the complexity offers practical opportunities for those who are willing to make the effort, enabling more appropriate targeting of services and products. This has implications for all financial services, for taxation policies, for social welfare and other government policy areas, as well as for commercial financial products. There are also implications for marriage guidance, for counselling, for fund-raisers, for lawyers, for mediators: anything or anyone who comes between 'me and my money'.

Implications for banking

The banking industry is the most obvious potential beneficiary of the insights gained from this exploration of personal money.

Banking takes place at an intersection between personal money and official, market money; between what could be called subjective and objective money. As I have demonstrated, the two speak quite different languages. Money in one is carrying unconscious and unspoken personal baggage, money in the other is supposed to be a straightforward medium of impersonal exchange. This basic difference in perspective, and in the language used, underpins misunderstandings and leads to feelings of anger, resentment and helplessness.

Financial institutions may seem to treat our money with less respect than is its due, trampling on delicate and intimate memories. Or, negative money memories may be transferred onto the bank, raising issues of control, for example, which go beyond the rational. Some people need the bank to be like a stern father, to help them control themselves, to stand between the individual and their childish impulses. Others deeply resent the dependence, the patronising tone, the continuing control. Still others may, unconsciously, both want the control and yet resent it. People often seem stuck in a sort of perpetual adolescence in their relationships with banks; this dependence and resentment leading to the petulant tone of much bank-bashing. A lot is irrational and it is independent of one's income. Enormously wealthy people are just as likely to be railing against a minor monthly bank fee as are those on low incomes. It is not the income that matters, it is the underlying psychosocial history of personal money. These irrational or emotional responses create particular ways of using specific banking services; they have practical consequences.

Banks cannot be expected to understand and respond to each idiosyncratic personal history. Nor are customers necessarily aware that these sorts of factors underlie their resentment of banks. Understanding that there *is* a history, that it may be delicate, and that the history remains relevant even if unconscious, should be fundamental knowledge for those in the field.

Understanding this context would also provide a competitive advantage.

It is particularly relevant at present as banks worldwide are restructuring their businesses in response to technological developments. They are rationalising branch networks, remodelling branches, changing the expectation of personal counter service to one of automated service. Banks, wisely, are trying a 'bob each way' by offering impersonal machine cubicles for those who want them, and some personalised service for others. The idea of mini-branch kiosks in supermarkets is a way of keeping an accessible human face, as well as linking banking to a more explicit commercialism. The research findings showed that the nature of the transaction does effect the banking method chosen. For example, ATMs were preferred for withdrawals, human tellers for deposits. Each method served particular psychological or unconscious needs, as we will see when we discuss saving.

The closure of branches in country towns has caused a groundswell of feeling, demonstrating all that is emotional about money. On top of practical considerations, such as convenience, symbolically people feel abandoned and even humiliated, as if their money isn't important enough to be taken seriously any longer. No matter how sincerely the banks try to convey that alternatives such as telephone banking can be just as convenient, people know that the changes are driven by bank-need, not customer-need. Smaller banks, which seem more customer-focused, have been successful in gaining market share and register higher customer-satisfaction levels than do the large banks.[2]

People have an interest in money in two senses of the word: they have legal ownership of the money, hence an entitlement to payment of interest, as well as a sense of their interests being at stake in a more personal way. They may not want to actually exercise their material or psychological interests, but they may like to have the legitimacy of that interest at least acknowledged. So-called 'private banking' departments within the large banks offer more personalised service for wealthier customers in an atmosphere of reverence and privacy, rather like club membership, with its air of privilege and belonging. This appears to recognise the personal nature of money, and accord it due seriousness, by allocating a particular person to take care of a customer's interests, discreetly, privately, and only if needed.

The struggle to keep money under control is a psychological as well as a physical fact that banks would do well to understand. Bank advertising sometimes acknowledges this need for personal control of money, stressing the way in which a new account can help you control your money. But the over-riding impression, at least as far as the major, large banks are concerned, can still appear to be control in the sense of power, exercised by the bank, rather than a partnership in assisting or facilitating the customer's own sense of personal control.

But it is difficult area. There is an almost instinctive scepticism about banks. And when others offer to help you control yourself, it can feel insulting, overbearing and intrusive. Self-doubt, the risk of being shamed or shown up, are never far from the surface. Suspicion of power (fathers, banks, playground bullies) may run deep, especially perhaps in Australia, where to be 'bossed around' may go against the national grain. Australian notions of egalitarianism tend towards 'thumbing a nose' at authority, at least in the rhetoric. Banks need to recognise some of these vagaries of personal money and the national psyche.

Financial institutions are operating now in a complex and often contradictory environment that makes relationships difficult. Ambivalence is inherent in money attitudes; there are the complications of personal predispositions, delicate personal money history, intimacy and secrecy. Changes, such as the move away from branches and further into automation, will not significantly alter people's fundamental predispositions concerning money.

Implications for saving

Though there are many other forms of saving, money in the bank is probably what most people think of as saving.[3] This is one step removed from the money box. Given the predispositional urges, the widespread parental encouragement to save, and the potential for pleasure in saving uncovered in my research, one would expect that Australians (of the Anglo-Celtic variety at least) may be a nation of savers. This is not the case. The household savings ratio has fallen over the past twenty years from 14.3 per cent in 1975 to a low of 2.4 per cent in 1995.[4] Though there are some signs of a small rise since then, OECD figures show that Australian savings rates are low compared with other similar economies: the 1997 household savings rates were 3.9 per cent in Australia, 11.1 per cent in the United Kingdom, 13.6 per cent in Japan.[5] The Federal government hectors us about the low level of national savings, and of per capita savings, and the need to rectify this situation; admonitions that sound very like parental ones. And, as with parental behaviour, government behaviour undermines the message. There is very little support for saving. Banks, instead, exhort us to borrow more, and they pay low interest rates on savings accounts.

There is also confusion about what constitutes saving, just as there is confusion about what constitutes debt. Schlomo Maital noted the high level of savings accounts in the United States, the fervent spoken commitment to saving, and yet the decreasing level of national savings and huge rise in consumer credit.[6] He suggests that people do not see outstanding credit-card balances as debt, and therefore can continue to chant anti-debt, pro-saving mantras in the face of contradictory personal behaviour. This seems to hold true for Australian society as well. The piety of the saving rhetoric espoused by adults, particularly to their children, is in marked contrast to the reality of adult behaviour.

The insights we have gained in this exploration of money attitudes could be used to assist in encouraging saving behaviour. For example, despite widespread use of electronic means for withdrawing money, many people still prefer to make deposits into the hands of a human being, rather than a machine. We like to withdraw money in private (using ATMs, avoiding guilt) but prefer to keep our deposits human (it seems more serious and safer). There is also a certain reassurance in being able to hold someone else responsible by 'handing it over' personally. If governments want to encourage saving, such depositing behaviour could be 'rewarded' by, at the very least, a metaphorical pat on the back. This may help reinforce, indeed reignite, dormant images of parental approval. If we want people to save, it should not be too hard to tap into basic attitudes to saving that are inherited from parents. Guilt about not saving is not far below the surface for most of us.

What percentage of the population is predisposed to save? What proportion are instinctive 'brakes', what proportion instinctive 'accelerators'? Such predispositions could be coopted into campaigns to support the savers. Rather than being made to seem mean, savers could be positioned as strong, clever, judicious. Positive incentives (material pats on the back) would help as well. At present there are confused messages about saving when deposits, and the interest earned on savings, are taxed. People are disproportionately irritated by taxes of this sort that feel like punishment for good behaviour.

Cash substitutes and global currencies

The transition to cashlessness could proceed more smoothly if basic attitudes to current money were understood. People are fond of cash: it holds memories — some bad, some good, some conscious, some not. It has a history and deep psychological resonances. These will linger: everyone born before the year 2000 (and possibly later) will have childhood cash memories that may become even more potent in its absence. There are many ways in which acceptance of currency changes could be facilitated. The money-imagery and money-memories revealed in this book could provide a substantial promotional foundation if carefully handled.

We uncovered the central importance of control issues, particularly in cash management. This key psychological variable needs to be harnessed in the transition to 'stored value cards' or 'smartcards'. The first reaction of some people, particularly with regard to something as primal as money, is to resist change, to almost deliberately not understand. Since money as we know it has emotional links to childhood, change can feel deeply threatening.

Piggy banks will not rattle when stuffed full of smartcards, nor will mother's purse bulge in quite the same way; smartcards won't go into the Christmas pudding; and countries that still have cash currencies will seem very exotic, albeit 'primitive'. There are opportunities for smartcard designers in all this. Some amounts of money may need to seem serious, others may need to feel personal. These emotional dimensions could be taken into the designers' lexicon. Rummaging through the cards in mother's purse might then continue to be an illicit pleasure of childhood.

The pressing need to 'control' money could be enhanced by appropriate design, and harnessed in campaigns to obtain acceptance of the new cash-substitute systems. Easy or 'smart' money may also seem potentially out of control. People may need to be assured that cash-substitute cards can service their need for control very well. My interviews with people showed that they do not automatically grasp this until it is explained in those terms. Careful investigation of alternative terminologies, graphic designs, marketing strategy and promotional content would be better managed if important underlying money attitudes, with all their fears and irrationalities, were understood.

The move towards a common currency has been a major

sticking point for European Union negotiators. At one stage in the process, newspapers reported more division at an EU meeting over currency than over nuclear testing.[7] There have been protests of some sort against the new currency in most of the affected nations, which is not surprising. If it is hard to reconcile the private money world within one culture to an official money world in that same culture, how much harder across cultural boundaries? The private imagery will vary in different countries. In addition, the perception of currency as psychologically precious, even if unacknowledged (perhaps more so if unacknowledged), will lead people to defend their own national currency and to be suspicious of others'. We invest a lot, emotionally, in our currency. To cross boundaries is problematic both literally and emotionally. It creates the potential for feelings of personal loss, and of loss of control, and this book has shown how important and ongoing is the struggle to keep control of money.

The move to cashlessness, to stored value cards, should help the global currency process. Cash-substitute cards might serve to 'neutralise' currency, divesting it of some of its personal and national characteristics. The process of 'Europeanising' or 'internationalising' may then be facilitated.

Taxation: a financial and emotional reckoning

Taxation is an example of the crossover territory between the personal experience of money and the official world of money. In the tax arena, the two discourses meet and often collide. As mentioned earlier in the book, many people reported great discomfort caused by this annual reckoning with representatives of 'official' money — when the subjective meets the objective. It is, on the surface, a financial reckoning but it has implications beyond assessing the balance between outgoings and incomings. Personal performance, personal values and priorities are revealed, and this can feel uncomfortable, even humiliating, for many people. At the most basic level, this is an annual exposure: something normally kept private has to be talked about and justified. The feeling of being 'judged', however inaccurate, is almost inevitable.

The Australian Taxation Office is trying to increase levels of voluntary compliance in paying personal and company tax. This is more than a matter of encouraging people to complete their own tax returns, and do it fully and honestly; rather, there is a desire to change the underlying attitude to taxation. A tax official suggested to me that many Australians have a 'Ned Kelly attitude' to tax, where to avoid paying is heroic. As cause or result, tax auditors, historically, have had an essentially combative attitude to eliciting and enforcing compliance. The new approach is supposed to be more of a partnership, encouraging the sense that tax is a contribution to society, made voluntarily rather than extracted unwillingly.

The self-assessment procedures now in operation, however, may have increased the level of anxiety. Under the old system, someone else took responsibility. Under the new system, the individual is handed responsibility — but may not feel up to it. Major questions of autonomy, control, dependence and independence are at issue here. The paternal, judgemental sense of the Taxation Office, and taxation accountants, working with you on your tax return was uncomfortable enough. That has now been replaced by self-assessment, subject to random audits. The 'big brother' feeling, that you may suddenly be jumped upon, might have introduced a note of punitive and random paternalism which is more unsettling than the old system.

There is also the troubling matter of equity: 'I'm happy to contribute as long as everyone else does equally.' In a voluntary system, there may be too much subjectivity and a hankering for objectivity: Who knows? Who controls? As we saw with money and banking, not everyone likes to be independent of father-figures. Judgements about how much to pay, how much to avoid or minimise, are likely to be coloured by greed and envy and shadowed by secrecy.

Privatisation: understanding the resistance

Some of the negative reaction to privatisation in Australia, particularly privatisation of fundamentals such as water or electricity, can be better understood in the context of the psychological centrality of control issues; specifically the fear of loss of control. Though government bureaucracies may be slow, impersonal and inefficient, they may seem preferable to the 'control' exacted by competing, and possibly rapacious, private interests. The effect on precariously balanced household budgets is the surface issue here, since people often assume privatisation will increase costs, despite the official claims that 'market forces' will reduce costs.

It is not just a financial matter, however, but also one of personal, psychological control over basic life elements. This area illustrates the gap between the economics discourse and the personal, each approaching the matter from a different perspective. The personal is based on fears, some rational and some irrational, of losing control while the official tries to persuade people that it is conferring greater control in the form of choice and competition. The personal attitude to control is also ambivalent. As was evident with banking, some people may not want to take control, or want others to mediate for them, and would prefer to cede control to government rather than to the unknown, often unaccountable, private sector. The extent to which such psychological complexities are at work in the debates about privatisation have been underestimated or ignored.

Divorce and gender differences

The implications of these findings for couples making a financial reckoning of their lives in order to come to a divorce settlement are obvious. There is the 'marriage money' to be negotiated as well as the baggage of 'his' money and 'her' money: each partner will be carrying from childhood, usually unconsciously, a personal history as well as an internal money predisposition, all operating under varying external social expectations. When a couple decides to divorce, it becomes obvious that money is not an impersonal, neutral medium of exchange. What is surprising is that we do not acknowledge this context outside of divorce. It is possible that healthier relationships in marriage may be negotiable if the personal story of money is at least acknowledged. If each partner were aware of their own orientation towards being essentially a saver or a spender, or somewhere in between, they could then work out a way to make family financial arrangements that went some way to satisfying each person's needs. Making more explicit some of the urges, the history and the discomfort, may be an effective prophylactic for any sort of partnership — domestic or business.

We have noted that women are likely to have memories of money that are connected to early important relationships, and often unhappy. Women have observed or absorbed complex emotional undercurrents, such as tensions between parents or sibling rivalries, more than was reported by men. If these tensions, consciously or unconsciously, are transferred to money itself then their attitudes to it are likely to be ambivalent. It indicates that women's ways of thinking about money contrast sharply with the way money is treated in the market-world, as something crisp and uncomplicated. This suggests directions for assisting women to deal with, and then put aside, negativity as a means to greater comfort with money. Some streams of the modern feminist movement have acknowledged that discomfort about money is a major impediment to women's advancement at senior levels in business and government. It can be, more broadly, an impediment to a general sense of competence and control.

Coming to terms with one's own money may help to develop money competence in the outside world. There are plenty of people, male and female, in responsible financial positions, whose personal money is subject to the sort of irrational, infantile, unthought-out positions that have been uncovered in this book. The private money ledger is often out of balance, either monetarily or psychologically.

Gambling

Out-of-balance money behaviour is seen at its worst in problem spending and problem gambling. My research set out specifically to focus on everyday 'normal' money, an area where there was only a little existing work. The special knowledge and particular issues associated with pathologies, such as problem gambling, seemed best left to others. Nonetheless, the insights derived from my investigation of money attitudes provide a basis for further study.

The 'control' variable, so central to money behaviour in general, is clearly central to gambling behaviour and, in particular, to uncontrolled or uncontrollable gambling. The difficult equilibrium, that of maintaining the saving–spending balance, then veers out of control. In Freudian terms, it seems likely that anal expulsives are more likely to be gamblers than anal retentives. The expulsives like to spread their money around and feel it is wasted if it is not active. Anal retentives, with their instinct to conserve, to hoard, seem less likely to gamble. However, it is possible that this hoarding predisposition is more prone to apparently uncharacteristic splurges — having been careful and retentive the floodgates suddenly open, releasing the pressure, the overwhelming nature of the urge frightening even themselves. An understanding of the characteristics of each predispositional orientation, and the concomitant urges, should help in diagnosis and therapy.

Psychological issues, such as obsessive-compulsive behaviour, locus of control, alienation and so on, will be tied up with underlying money predispositions and psychosocial history. In more general terms, the fantasies surrounding gambling are an extension of the whole infantile omnipotent fantasy, the wishfulness, the Kleinian 'inexhaustible breast'. The tendency to 'magic gestures' is played out at casinos and poker machine venues around the world. The official language of the gambling industry indulges in a little sleight of hand — it calls itself 'gaming' rather than 'gambling', as if by dropping two letters the activity is rendered innocently playful.

These are just a few examples of the practical benefits of recognising and reconciling personal money with official money. The final chapter will now revisit the secrecy surrounding money, uncovering what our money-language reveals and why we feel such shame.

11

The Secret Life of Money

Is money really 'the last emotional taboo in our society', as psychotherapist, David Krueger, claims?[1] It's hard to believe when there is so much talk about money. Most of the talk, however, keeps money at arm's length: it's about other people's money, the rich, the poor, how to make it, how to lose it, banking, economics, accountancy, taxation. On these subjects there is endless talk. But *my* money is a different matter. Personal money is private.

Money is full of contradictions. There is the talk and yet the silence. And, despite the silence, money is also a powerful projective device. If you ask someone about their attitudes to money it can expose the deepest aspects of their personality, which is precisely why we resist the subject; we have a sense, largely unconscious, that it might show too much. Not least, it might reveal the extent of our irrationality, the unthought-out nature of our money attitudes.

We are stuck with this ambivalence, constantly seeking to balance money's many facets. There is no singularity about money and no single answer to what money is or what it represents. Economic anthropologists Russell Belk and Melanie Wallendorf conclude that 'in contemporary society, money represents a tension, a co-existing inconsistency between sacred and profane, and between good-sacred and evil-sacred'.[2] Governments capitalise (literally) on this ambivalence by linking sacred with profane: in Australia, an environment policy is linked to the sale of the government-owned communications carrier, Telstra; funds for public libraries and hospitals are raised from gambling revenue.

From a Freudian starting point, the contradictions contained in money begin with retention versus elimination. Then we see evasion versus projection; prudery versus prurience; repulsion versus fascination; saving versus spending. In gender terms, money is symbolised sometimes by male potency, sometimes by mother's milk. The femaleness of everyday money contrasts with the maleness of official money. Perhaps money is a hermaphrodite. It has been suggested that the capacity of money to breed money, its interest-bearing ability, does make it self-reproducing.[3]

Money is a symbol, and symbols often contain both positive and negative aspects. The dualism inherent in money is not a clash of opposites but rather two sides of the same coin. Money will continue to have both a public life and a private life. To reach the private life of money we have to break through the secrecy. We also need to understand its causes.

The secrets, the secrecy, the shame

There are five main secrets about money. The first — and it is a deceptively simple one — is that money does indeed have a private life. It is kept buried by most of us and, significantly, is unrecognised or denied by the world of official money. The second is that we do carry mental baggage from childhood that directly affects our adult money attitudes and behaviours. The third is that we have a basic predisposition or orientation, existing probably from infancy, to be essentially savers or spenders. The fourth is the extent of the secrecy itself — we don't even talk about the fact that we avoid the subject of our personal money. The fifth is that our income level doesn't make much difference to any of the other four.

Money is basically something we deal with alone. One person, quoted earlier in the book, described money as 'awesome in its secrecy'. Over three-quarters of my interview subjects did not know their own parents' income, and three-quarters said their children did not, in turn, know *their* incomes. Other studies have shown similar patterns of reticence. It may still be considered 'bad manners' to talk about money even when other similar strictures on behaviour have long since been jettisoned. When it comes to the central question 'How much are you worth?' the silence is deafening.

My findings, and Jan Pahl's in Britain, cast some doubt on the extent to which couples share their personal money lives or thoughts. Sixteen per cent of my interviewees confessed to a bank account kept secret from their spouse. (Is the incidence of secret accounts increasing as the incidence of joint accounts increases?) Others may have a separate account that is not a secret but they prefer not to reveal the actual amount in the account to partner or spouse. In Pahl's research, the majority of spouses knew more or less how much the other earned, but 16 per cent of wives and 32 per cent of husbands did not know their partner's income from the primary paid work. While it was not actually kept secret — they felt they could find out if they wanted to — the level of secrecy increased for income from second or 'extra' jobs.[4]

Researchers avoid the money subject, so there is little data to call on. The complexity of the topic and the interconnection of variables do make it a difficult research area. Evasion is also common in therapy: 'The patient and therapist can implicitly collude to maintain the taboo against the discussion of money, fees, collection, and feelings generated by money.'[5] 'Could it be that psychoanalysts shared with society a reluctance to talk about something that revealed too many hidden personal hopes and fears?'[6] I once commented to a visiting therapist that many people feel agonised when obliged to discuss personal money with accountants or bank managers. 'Oh?' he queried. 'I thought *I* was the only one!' Another claimed he had not realised the extent of his own, and his patients', evasion of money questions until he read parts of the thesis on which this book is based. It had prompted him to reappraise his handling of fees, to become more upfront about his need to be paid for what he does.

Reticence is self-reinforcing; because people are unaccustomed to talking about money among themselves there is no routine language for the subject. Thus, as Jan Pahl also noted, the discourse about money tends to comprise anecdote, comparison, projection. The meaning is contained in stories and anecdotes, and though they may seem like diversions from the main subject, they are in fact the personal money-subject in disguise.

Why do disguises seem necessary? It remains surprising that money, with which many say society is obsessed, should still be surrounded by such coyness. Money is like nudity. It requires a certain equivalence or it verges on obscenity. A sense of potential exposure, social and psychological, underlies the reticence about money.

How can we understand this fear of being exposed? Psychoanalytic theory, especially Erik Erikson's work, is useful as it returns us to the central question of control. Erikson described eight psychosocial ages in our development.[7] The second age he described as 'Autonomy *v.* Shame and Doubt'. Autonomy involves feeling in control. Its opposite, the lack of a sense of control, can lead to self-doubt and shame. This coincides with the anal stage of development, the stage involving holding on and letting go. As young children learn to deal with these opposing urges, key people in their environment provide (or not) protection against 'meaningless and arbitrary experiences of shame and of early doubt'.

'Shame is an emotion insufficiently studied, because in our civilization it is so early and easily absorbed by guilt. Shame supposes that one is completely exposed and conscious of being looked at: in one word, self-conscious. One is visible and not ready to be visible; which is why we dream of shame as a situation in which we are stared at in a condition of incomplete dress, in night attire, "with one's pants down".' Erikson goes on to say: 'Doubt is the brother of shame.' Doubt creeps up from behind, literally and metaphorically, and in adult pathological form can turn into paranoia. He adds: 'Adults, and seemingly mature and unneurotic ones, display a sensitivity concerning a possible shameful "loss of face" and fear of being attacked "from behind" which is ... highly irrational and in contrast to the knowledge available to them.'

In Chapter 4 I described American research by Wernimont and Fitzpatrick into the meanings of money. The major category of money-meaning which emerged from responses in that study was dubbed by the researchers 'shameful failure'. They said: 'Money seems to mean something that is, potentially at least, an indication of failure and a source of embarrassment and degradation.'[8] It gets us closer to understanding why exposing one's financial affairs to accountants or bank managers might feel humiliating. In Erikson's terms, it feels a bit like being caught with your pants down.

The word 'shame' keeps creeping into money stories. An acquaintance discovered, after her father's death, that he had for years been borrowing the money to continue paying dividends from the family company to his wife and children. He had continued in this well-meant deception to avoid the shame of his business failure being exposed, to avoid loss of face. Ironically the cover-up seemed as childishly incompetent in the eyes of others as he had feared the original business failure would. And his family were left feeling doubly bad, bearing shame on his behalf, and shame that money and failure were too private, too painful, for him to share with them. A spate of executive suicides in Japan over business failures is also attributed to shame, to a deep sense of having failed families and employees.

A friend recently sold his house for less than he believed it was worth. He became very depressed and said that he felt ashamed. Why would he feel ashamed? The result hadn't affected anyone but himself. Disappointed maybe. Perhaps angry with those who may have led him to expect more. Or angry with himself for being unrealistic, or for being greedy. But shame? Erikson's theories suggest it stems from a perceived failure of control resulting in a diminished sense of himself as a competent person. Despite making a modest profit, he felt exposed and beset by self-doubt.

There are, of course, people who lose their own money, and other people's money, yet feel no apparent shame. They may feel they are more grown-up, more worldly than the rest of us, less constrained: 'So you win some you lose some.' They may be better evaders, deniers, as well as predisposed spenders. But they often find excuses and scapegoats that sound similar to the child's justification for stealing from mother's purse: 'It isn't fair, I didn't get tuckshop money or pocket money like the others did.' In essence their behaviour connects to the idea of infantile omnipotence frustrated and pursuit of a fantasy of inexhaustible supply.

Wealth and shame are sometimes unhappy partners. I recently read a collection of interviews with heirs and was interested to see how frequently they used the phrase 'I felt ashamed'.[9] I had expected that some might feel guilt about inheriting money when there is so much poverty, or when the money was obtained on the basis of another's efforts, not their own. But shame seemed a slightly puzzling emotion. When I followed it up with some Australian heirs they explained that they did feel shame. It was connected to the secrecy, the feeling that money occupied dark corners of their childhoods. They weren't always sure how ethically it had been made. In addition, some had suffered severe emotional neglect in childhood, or family dysfunction more often associated with extreme poverty. They felt they could not ask for, nor expect, sympathy, and they often felt incompetent and inadequate about their lack of money knowledge, all of which caused considerable self-doubt and shame.

People on low incomes also avoid 'exposing' themselves. We have already noted the contagiousness of poverty and the tendency of those on lower incomes to describe themselves as middle income. They avoided using the phrase 'we can't afford it', not because it wasn't true, but because it felt too shaming, as if it would reveal to their children their lack of success or competence in generating funds. People from families that had experienced a significant downturn in family finances during their childhoods were less likely to have talked with parents about money than were those in families that had experienced a financial change for the better. Lower-income people generally avoided talking about their personal money in case it was interpreted as 'crying poor' or bleating: **'You don't talk about it because you don't want to embarrass other people and at the same time you'd be embarrassing yourself, or seem to be making an issue out of something that's no big deal.'** In Australia, where the rhetoric of egalitarianism exerts a powerful influence, not to be a 'whinger' is as important as not getting 'above yourself' or 'up yourself'.

Extremes of income are not required for us to keep money quiet. We all fear the shame of exposing ourselves. We assume others are more competent, less irrational than we are. We avoid the shame of exposing the extent of our immaturity regarding money, the extent of our reflex, parent-parodying platitudes.

Is money dirty?

Why do adults still hesitate to ask their own parents how much was spent on a car? Or ask a friend how much a new television cost? This sort of awkwardness about money remains puzzling, despite rational explanations about social comparison and convention, or inequalities of power and control.

The evasiveness might vindicate the Freudian view of money as excrement, something dirty. This is reflected in the language of money that is so much part of the vernacular as to pass largely unrecognised, at least consciously. 'Dirty' (criminal) money gets 'laundered' to turn it into 'clean' (legal) money. People taken down financially are 'taken to the cleaners'. Money success is referred to as hitting 'paydirt'. The descriptions 'filthy rich' and 'dirty capitalist' are commonplace. Although the expression 'dirt poor' puts the economic position plainly, to be 'filthy rich' makes riches sound even dirtier than poverty.

In the vernacular, too, are expressions which connect money more directly with excrement. To be very mean is to be 'tightarsed'; 'pots of money' and 'to make your pile' are slightly more ambiguous; while one wonders if economists or accountants notice that 'the bottom line' constitutes a Freudian *double entendre*. The new Australian $50 bill was initially referred to as 'the baby's nappy' due to its muddy colouring. Even Keynes' description of the pleasurable anticipation created by abstinence or deferral can fit into the Freudian model of anal retentive pleasure.

ATMs are widely referred to in Australia as 'holes in the wall'. One of my interviewees described money flowing from ATMs 'like an endless roll of toilet paper', reinforcing the faecal imagery, as does 'loose' change and 'I'm a bit of a softie with money'. It is possible that anal retentives, like Elisabeth and Neil in the case studies, prefer plastic cards because they are not only orderly but also 'cleaner' than cash.

In his book *Money, Language and Thought*, Marc Shell explores the 'money of the mind': 'Recognising money of the mind involves locating monetary form in linguistic exchange ... My argument is not that money is talked about in particular works of literature and philosophy (which is certainly the case), but that money talks in and through discourse in general.'[10]

The chart on page 183 lists some commonly used expressions about money. Through everyday expressions such as these, language operates as a mirror of attitudes, both absorbing and reflecting often unconscious images and thought processes. In *The Rhetoric of Economics*, Donald McCloskey says: 'Figures of speech are not mere frills. They think for us.'[11] Two main points should be noted about everyday money language. The first is its colour and tone, the way it ranges from virtue, piety and purity through to dirt and disgust. The second is the marked contrast between such everyday expressions, in common use, and the language of money in the official, or economics, discourse — displayed in the chart on page 185.

The contrast beween the language of the two areas is striking. Economics, banking and accounting have largely opted for mathematical models and the language of the material and physical sciences; their terminology being impersonal, detached, technical. The words are often neutral or, by virtue of being part of a pair, they are effectively neutralised, as in mathematical equations. The language helps to construct the sense of a scientific discipline. Discipline is an appropriate word for this very 'straight-backed' discourse. The brevity, the detached nature of the jargon, keeps it well away from the murky depths of personal meaning we have uncovered. Thus the government will set up an 'expenditure review committee', which everyone knows is a euphemism for slashing of departmental budgets. An 'audit' may be a thoroughly unsettling financial inquisition, but the neutrality of the language keeps it distant from racks and thumbscrews.

Everyday money language

Sacred
- pennies from heaven
- almighty dollar
- forgiving debt

Motherhood/Orality/Food
- lap of luxury
- milking the cash cow
- nest egg
- feathering your nest
- money hungry
- expensive tastes
- to coin a phrase
- for love or money
- bread/breadwinner
- dough
- money for jam
- chips/when the chips are down
- money speaks/talks
- put your money where your mouth is
- milked for money

Organic/Nature
- doesn't grow on trees
- windfall
- husbanding resources
- bottomless pit

Circulation/Flow
- blood money
- splashing money around
- pooling resources/into the common pool
- a reservoir of cash
- not the full shilling
- cash flow

Hands/Touch/Tactile
- cash in hand
- handling money
- put it away so I can't touch it
- throw money at the problem
- a soft touch
- touch me for money

Morality/Sexuality
- loose money
- easy money
- modest means

Diminish
- embarrassment of riches
- modest means
- money isn't everything
- a small fortune
- petty cash
- it's only money
- hush money
- retiring debt
- a bob each way
- on the never-never

Anality/Dirt
- filthy lucre
- filthy rich
- stinking rich
- dirt poor
- filthy capitalist
- dirt cheap
- to make your pile
- taken to the cleaners
- loose change
- a softie with money
- cold hard cash
- pots of money
- tight arse
- cash cushion
- money laundering
- dirty money/clean money
- wallowing in money
- shooting crap
- money-grubber
- slush fund

Virtuous/Pure → Natural metaphors → Dirty/Disgusting

Some interesting exceptions include the words 'withdrawal' and 'loss', both with significant emotional connotations in addition to their physical meanings. The word 'interest' can refer to proprietorial and legal interest as well as to pleasurable preoccupation and personal involvement. A 'credit squeeze' has a lively palpability, while continuing use of the biblical expression 'forgiving debt' keeps this at the good and pious end of economic activity. The word 'depression' has vivid mental meaning which parallels its topographical and meteorological meanings. Its adoption by economists denotes its appearance on their graphs as a physical declivity but its emotional and atmospheric meanings are equally low.

In 1996, Kerry Packer, described as 'Australia's richest man', sold a 15 per cent stake in Melbourne's casino for $204 million. The company statement to the Stock Exchange said the sale was 'motivated by the wish to liquefy some of its assets for use in other transactions'.[12] The detached sound of the language in this official statement keeps money quarantined from disturbing complexities, keeps it firmly under control. To acknowledge other possible motives for the sale — power? greed? acquisitiveness? envy? omnipotence? Oedipal rivalry? — would be too exposing.

By contrast, the colourful language and images of the personal, everyday money discourse unwittingly display the potentially disturbing side of money. The two discourses are so far apart that it is difficult to see reconciliation. Yet perhaps separation serves a purpose and there is no need for a reconciliation. It may be precisely the function of the everyday discourse to keep it separate, beyond the reach of those who would measure and dissect, to keep it *mine*, even beyond the prying gaze of therapists. So we can move from one discourse to the other as it suits: when we want our money to feel under control, we can adopt the language of balance sheets and accounts rendered. When we want it to be ours, when we want it to teach our children something about important values and

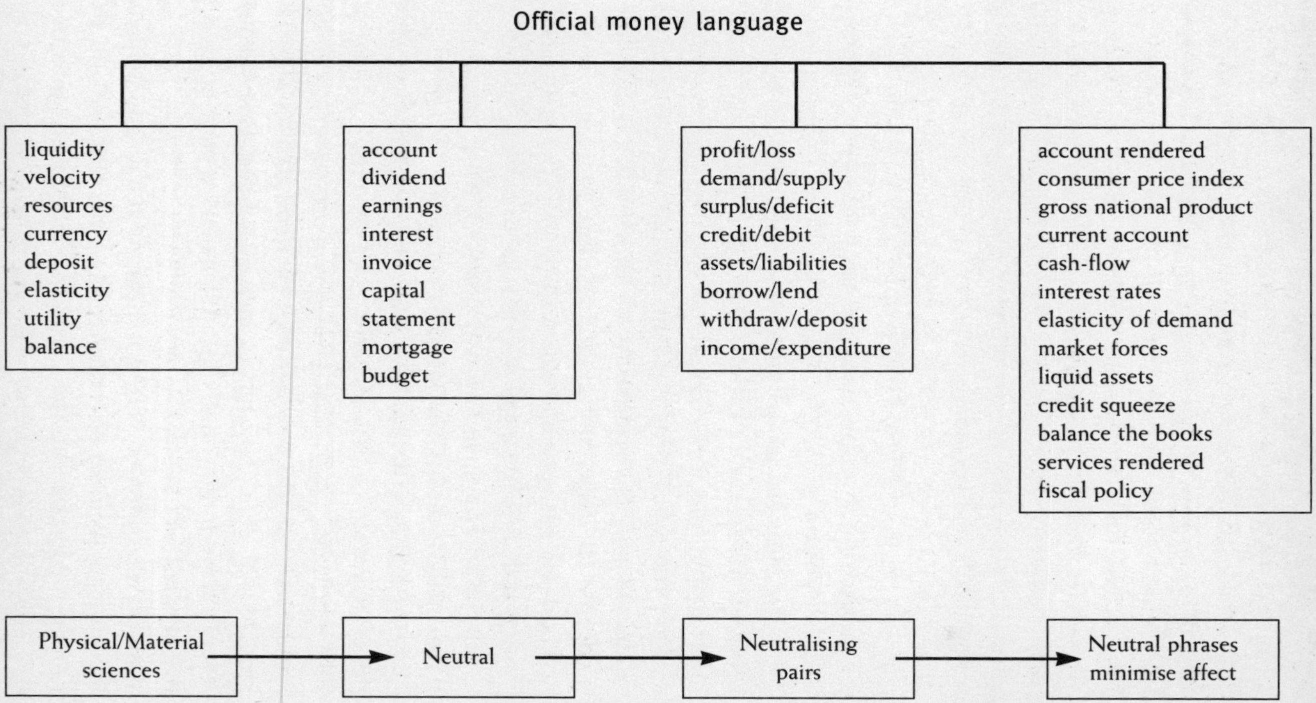
Official money language
liquidity
velocity
resources
currency
deposit
elasticity
utility
balance
account
dividend
earnings
interest
invoice
capital
statement
mortgage
budget
profit/loss
demand/supply
surplus/deficit
credit/debit
assets/liabilities
borrow/lend
withdraw/deposit
income/expenditure
account rendered
consumer price index
gross national product
current account
cash-flow
interest rates
elasticity of demand
market forces
liquid assets
credit squeeze
balance the books
services rendered
fiscal policy
Physical/Material sciences
Neutral
Neutralising pairs
Neutral phrases minimise affect

attitudes, then we use the colourful imagery of the everyday, personal discourse.

As this book has shown, people do use money to carry all sorts of unspoken things because they know it has power. Money does 'speak' in both senses: it has impact on our children because they recognise its economic worth. It is because it speaks to them in this sense that it can also function as a potent carrier for values and priorities that go well beyond the narrowly economic. This is money's double value: to speak economically and personally.

Money speaking silently

A combination of unconscious and conscious early influences — predispositions together with childhood experiences — forms the basis of our attitudes to money in adulthood. In *Money and Mind*, Edward Hallowell and William Grace say:

> The emotional meaning of money to any one person may have roots that twist and turn through the past and the unconscious as circuitously and mysteriously as any other deeply felt issue, and getting at those roots may require abundant patience and imagination. Most people have a rich and complex set of associations to money, full of displaced meaning, rife with the most intense affects, and guarded by a host of dogged defences.[13]

Since money attitudes have their roots in childhood when money-talk was avoided, the silence leaves a feeling that, not only was money unspoken, it was also somehow unspeakable. People pick up this message in childhood and continue to struggle with its consequences in adulthood. Psychoanalytic theories about money firmly locate the development of money attitudes not just in infancy, but in intimacy. Money emerges from the space between child and parent as a deeply personal and intimate medium of exchange. It is this that explains the secrecy, the furtiveness, the coyness and the fierce protectiveness. It is this that explains the painful fear of exposure.

It is also this that leads to money's attraction, a fascination with the forbidden, to both the prudery and the prurience. Interest in money has a sensual aspect — it resembles passionate interest in food or sex, or even the wary fascination with death. This, in turn, cements the secrecy, causes the taboo. So we have money–excrement–dirt–secrecy–shame and money–nurture–sensuality–potency–sexuality as contexts, all of which accounts for the shock of money outside the boundaries of 'a certain propriety'. These boundaries are hard to pinpoint because the inherent secrecy and contradictoriness result in a narrow pathway for 'acceptable' money behaviour. Even more difficult to negotiate are the pathways that connect one person's version of what is acceptable with another's. Individuals have different experiences and different internal predispositions. Pathways must be forged through these idiosyncratic and sometimes delicate personal perspectives. With people of unequal status, or income, communication is further complicated. And since the landscape is unexplored, unspoken and secret, there are no maps.

Money speaks by revealing the person within. Money speaks by conveying messages to children about values beyond pecuniary value. Money speaks by controlling others. Money also speaks the language of material, market exchange. It is a very talkative substance. This book has articulated its non-material voices — money speaking about our pasts, about our values, our hopes and our fears. Ironically, as we have seen, it often speaks silently, and perhaps more powerfully for that very silence. The 'taken for granted' nature of money has been confronted and personal money revealed in a way that confounds its narrow market definition as an impersonal medium of exchange. We have uncovered the formative layers of our adult money-attitudes. From this psychosocial perspective money acts as a crucible in a mix of internal predispositions, continuing childhood influences, social conventions and economic realities.

This has been one way of looking at money. It is an important beginning, but there is much more to discover. What proportion of us are, by basic orientation, primarily spenders, what proportion savers? What about other cultural groups? Are predispositions likely to transcend cultural barriers, as they have been shown to transcend income levels? What effect, if any, will cashlessness have on such orientations? Will the cautious messages that we continue to pass on to our children change as circumstances change? A recent report indicated a change in emphasis, saying that Australians 'save what is left over from spending, instead of spending what is left over from saving'.[14] Will behavioural change drag some aspects of underlying money attitudes along with it or will there continue to be a disjunction between action and words?

The desire for 'an answer' to what money means is part of the wishfulness that surrounds money, the infantile fantasy. It leads to the hope that a solution can be grabbed from the shelf; that by organising the wallet, for example, or visiting a money guru, we can tame money by 'knowing' money. Hence the success of money 'how to' books, the lure of lottery tickets and of 'get rich quick' schemes. The fantasy of omnipotence is pivotal to understanding this quest. The search for an 'inexhaustible breast' may underpin gambling behaviour, the dream of coins spilling endlessly from a poker machine. The fear (subconscious) of this fantasy in our children is what leads to its countervailing mottos: 'We can't afford it' or 'I'm not a bottomless pit'. To deny the fantasy before it gets out of hand, to keep it under control, is at the core of much that we have explored in this money-journey.

As money becomes more abstract, understanding its underpinnings may be even more important. In a review of a book on money, British writer and literary critic Frank Kermode pointed out that when lives are lived increasingly on credit, money becomes more 'an affair of the imagination', more poetic.[15] If money itself is intangible and, in addition, our basic attitudes to it remain secret and unacknowledged, then the risks of unrealistic fantasies getting out of control increase. The collapse of big businesses, from Christopher Skase to Barings Bank, shows what can happen when people forget, or choose to ignore, that money is something real that can be lost. Casinos deliberately foster this sense of unreality by issuing plastic tokens in place of real cash. When money feels like toy money then we risk dangerous replays of the cavalier extravagances of childhood Monopoly games.

Everyone has a personal money psycho-history, even those who are most at ease in the world of impersonal, market money. To develop an awareness of our own basic orientation to money, and an understanding of the baggage we carry from our childhood, may help to liberate us from some of the irrational aspects of our money attitudes and behaviours. A reconciliation of the personal money balance sheet might mean that unconscious, essentially infantile responses move aside in favour of a more adult sense of control of this most complex medium. In our society, money is both necessary for, and a symbol of, maturity and independence. As with emotional maturity, financial maturity may require acknowledgement of the past. This will be increasingly necessary in times of rapid financial change, enormous pressures to spend and the rise in gambling opportunities.

Once we balance our own books, then we can move to balancing the subjective ledger with the objective ledger: *my* money with *their* money, personal money with official market money. What we have seen in this exploration of money is a picture of economic irrationality, a picture at odds with the prevailing official embrace of economic rationalism. It is not a picture derived from a bunch of cranks or money neurotics. This is a snapshot of normal Australians of all incomes, most of whom occupy responsible positions around the country. In addition, they are running households and are forging the money attitudes and behaviours of the next generation. Like it or not, money has an interior life that affects, on a daily basis, the way we approach our exterior lives. It is far better to have money's secret life on the table rather than under the table… or under the bed.

Appendix: The Research Method and Sample

The qualitative research approach

The research underpinning this book was essentially qualitative in nature. This means that it was based on lengthy interviews with people individually or in groups (known as focus groups). In this sort of research one is listening to the opinions expressed as well as trying to uncover the attitudes, beliefs, emotions that underlie or are attached to those opinions. This includes observation of the words people use, the moods, silences, body language and so on, all aiming to build up a picture that increases our understanding. The benefit of qualitative research is that it is flexible enough to follow up unexpected leads, and it is sensitive to nuances and paradoxes.

Statistical, or quantitative, research, is essential when large samples are required and/or when the data to be obtained is straightforward. It is not good at dealing with ambiguity and contradiction, which are characteristic of money attitudes. Numerically-oriented people find the qualitative method too subjective. Statistics look more objective — though they may not be. In his book *The Rhetoric of Economics*, Donald McCloskey points out that so-called 'hard' data can be as much subject to rhetorical flourish, distortion and embellishment as the so-called 'soft' data of non-statistical research.[1]

I have spent almost 30 years conducting attitude-research projects for marketing, political and social research purposes. My academic background is in political sociology and political psychology. For the doctoral project on which this book is based I was enrolled at the University of Melbourne's Business School, an appropriate place, I thought, to look closely at money.

The PhD project

In practical terms, how did the project evolve? The first year of a PhD program is spent in reading widely all that is available on the topic: books, journals, research reports and so on. Since mine was to be a cross-disciplinary project, the reading task was particularly broad, ranging across economics, sociology, anthropology, psychology and psychoanalytic studies. This process enables the precise subject of the research to be more finely tuned: gaps in knowledge are identified, hypotheses developed. At the same time, one begins to plan the way the practical details will be organised: Who will be interviewed, and by what method? Questionnaires, individual face-to-face interviews, focus groups? These are major decisions, and the selected sample and method have to be supported by strong academic rationales.

While pondering these decisions, I was attentive to all the money-talk that goes on in the course of daily life. I began to ask people more specifically, but informally, about their money attitudes. Once, we were at a friend's house for a Melbourne Cup Day lunch, I was asked which horse I had backed in my annual little flutter. I reported that I'd put an each-way bet on a certain horse. 'Each-way bet?' said my host incredulously.

'What would you bother to do that for? You either think something's going to win or you don't.' I thought about this difference between us and realised that it signified a vast difference in our attitudes, not only to money and risk, but to many other aspects of life as well.

I wondered whether people for whom money is work — who deal with money on a daily and routine basis — would have different attitudes from the rest of us. I had a useful discussion with a futures trader, successfully making money for himself and others. This man was interesting because he knew a lot about the psychology of investment, in what makes markets rise and fall and what makes people jump in or bail out. Despite his interest in the motivation of others, he was uncomfortable talking about himself. On another tack, I talked at length with a person who had been 'done out of' an inheritance by a stepmother who sounded archetypically wicked in this version of the saga. It produced fascinating insights into money and family politics, sex-role expectations and the darker side of money — its capacity to wound from beyond the grave.

The formal research: individual and group interviews

Though these money stories were helpful and interesting I decided that the (apparent) ordinariness of more 'normal' and non-expert money lives was the territory I wanted to explore. I began by conducting five pilot interviews, a fairly standard procedure for a research journey such as this. Initial interviews help to establish the parameters of people's talk: What are the dimensions of the subject? How do people react to certain prompts from me? What seems to work, or not work, in terms of encouraging discussion?

After the pilot interviews, I set up six focus-group discussions. A research focus group typically consists of six to eight people who come to a specified location for a discussion on a broadly specified topic. The discussions last about two hours, and participants are usually paid something for their attendance. To choose this method for the central part of the research raised some questions. The research literature had described secrecy surrounding money — the idea of money as 'the last taboo'. So would it work? Would it be feasible to get people to talk frankly about something as important and personal as money, in a group context? In the 30-odd years in which I have been using the focus-group research method, I have often been asked to explore personal, and potentially uncomfortable, subjects in groups. My experience has been that the group-of-strangers environment may 'free up' talk in a way that the intensity of a one-on-one interview may not.

In addition to the possibility of greater candour, the group method builds a larger sample in a shorter time than can individual interviews. The group dynamic itself stimulates ideas and offers opportunity, as the group reacts and interacts, to gauge the strength, the intensity, the flexibility of those ideas. Attitudes and opinions can thus be explored as part of a social dynamic. This seemed particularly appropriate given the nature of the topic. Money is deeply personal and at the same time intrinsically social — exchange and interaction being at its core.

The focus-group moderator facilitates and guides the discussion, ensuring that each area of interest is covered and that every participant can contribute. Participants must feel assured that their contribution will be treated with respect, both during the discussions and later. For this reason, identities have been well disguised in the book, and in some cases, a composite picture is presented — an amalgam of individuals sharing a particular way of looking at things. Nevertheless, the people in the book, and their experiences, will seem familiar. We can all recognise ourselves in other people's money stories.

The interview sample

After selecting the focus-group method, decisions had to be made as to group composition. Who would be in the groups? The first decision was about gender. I decided that, of the six groups, three would comprise all men and three comprise all women. I decided to segregate the discussions for several reasons: men and women may speak different 'languages' about money; women may still 'defer' to men in this area; and they may, at the very least, have differing priorities. On the whole, it has been found that people are more comfortable talking in relatively homogeneous group settings.

For similar reasons, I specified three different income levels and held discussions with each level separately. The lower-income group was defined as pre-tax annual household incomes below $30 000; middle-income as pre-tax household incomes in the range $35 000–$50 000; upper-income was defined as above $90 000 annually, pre-tax. The basis for these income levels came from Australian Bureau of Statistics figures as well as income breaks used by ANZ Bank market researchers. The intention, however, was not a representative sample but rather to set up distinct income 'splits' in order to make more visible any differences in attitudes between income levels.

Gender and income, therefore, were the main research variables: two groups, one all male, one all female, at each of three income levels. Other potential variables were held constant: all participants were aged 35–55 years, married, and had at least one child aged under sixteen and living at home. All were Anglo-Celtic in backgound and in all cases the main household income-earner was currently in employment. The rationale for this was that I wanted to explore inter-generational attitudes. By selecting people in mid-age and with children still at home, people would be able to reflect on their own childhoods as well as talk about their current child-rearing practices. By selecting married participants, from households in which someone was in full-time employment, the particular money experience of divorce or unemployment was deliberately sidelined. Nevertheless, several participants had experience of one or other, or both, divorce and unemployment.

It was necessary to focus on a specific cultural group because attitudes to money may vary from one culture to another. Anglo-Celts still make up the largest cultural group in Australia and much of Australian institutional life still reflects these origins.[2] For the purposes of my focus-group recruitment I specified that respondents were to have been born in Australia themselves and with both parents of British stock. It would be fascinating to repeat the formal part of the investigation among people of different cultural backgounds. It should be said, however, that in the years spent researching this subject, I have talked to many people from different cultural backgounds and this has contributed to the overall picture.

The people who took part in the focus groups were recruited for me by a firm which specialises in respondent recruitment for research purposes. I provided a list of specifications — the sample details I have already described — and people turned up at the appointed time at a venue also supplied by the recruiting firm. The recruiter was instructed to exclude people who work, or had worked, in the Australian Taxation Office or Social Security, to pre-empt any fears about confidentiality in discussions. Also excluded were people who worked in financial fields in any capacity.

Participants were told they would be taking part in a discussion about money and that it was not a market research project. This might have produced people who were more comfortable with money, or at least comfortable talking about money. They could have been atypical in the sense that anyone really reluctant to talk about money may have excluded themselves. If that were so, however, it makes even more significant the continuing privacy and secrecy that the research uncovered. Other researchers have pointed out that there is a tendency to 'happy' money functioning: those in dysfunctional money situations may be unlikely to participate in projects such as this. It is also possible that the 'saving' position may have been over-represented, for similar reasons: people who are 'good' with money (i.e. who feel they have money under control) may have been more likely to attend discussions.

It was interesting that, despite my using the word 'money' in all my verbal and written communications with the recruiting firm, the organiser referred to the project as 'finance' on her own internal communications and on my account, avoiding that 'money' word. The out-of-pocket costs associated with this commercial recruiting were met by the ANZ Bank. It was a generous gesture as the contribution came with no strings attached, other than priority access to the findings. From their point of view, it was a very cheap (cost price) insight into the minds of their market.

A further dimension to the project was provided by the chance to conduct research workshops in Melbourne and Brisbane with small groups of wealthy women. These women had annual pre-tax incomes ranging from $100 000 to $1 million. At the bottom end of this income scale were two young respondents in their twenties. Most of the others were in the middle-age range (35–55), while two were in their sixties. Their cultural backgounds varied widely. Very little money research has had access to attitudes of the very wealthy so this inclusion has enriched the project. In summary, the 'official' research sample looked like this:

	Male	*Female*	*Total*
Pilot interviews	2	3	5
Focus groups (6 groups)			
2 × Lower-income	7	8	15
2 × Middle-income	7	9	16
2 × Upper-income	7	6	13
Wealthy women	–	12	12
Total	23	38	61

That was the formal part of my research. However, informal discussions with friends, colleagues and strangers constantly added variety to the input. Media interviews, newspaper articles, novels, conversations overheard in trams and in shops — all provided material that added value to the overall picture. I did not see these as incidental to, or less important than, the main task of the formal research interviews. These were examples of money-attitudes-in-action, noted carefully and incorporated into the findings, in much the same way as the participant-observer in sociological/anthropological research builds up a total picture via the meshing of multiple strands and viewpoints.

Some quantitative information was also obtained from participants in the six main focus groups, who were asked to complete a questionnaire before discussions commenced. This served several purposes. I couldn't be sure in advance whether people would feel comfortable discussing money openly in a group. The questionnaire provided an opportunity for people to set down private information. It also gave me a record of those private responses before the influence of others came into play. It allowed me later to compare the private notes with the public utterances of group members. Finally, the more numerical questions enabled some limited quantification of findings. The sample comprised 44 respondents (the people in the six focus groups). Since the sample is small, this data was used to illustrate and support the qualitative findings rather than as an end in itself.

Discussion format

My focus groups began with people completing the questionnaire. Then we talked about early memories of money. Most people could come up with a personal story about money in childhood, which proved a good 'way in' to the sort of personal money territory I was wanting to explore. We talked specifically about the way in which money was treated in their childhoods, as a topic and as a substance — what was said, what was not said, what was done, what they thought their parents were seeking to convey about money. About half way through the discussions, people completed another questionnaire ('when I think about money I feel ...') containing a semantic differential scale.[3] This consisted of a 5-point scale on a continuum between pairs of words such as 'warm–cold'; 'private–public'; 'exciting–dull'; 'in control–out of control'; 'tense–relaxed'. The order and rotation of the scales were varied in each group to avoid any order biases. The scale provided a vehicle for people to articulate feelings and introduced some common, explicit emotional language into the discussion. We then moved on to people's current money behaviour — how they organise it, how they feel about currency, what they say to their own children, what they do about pocket money, restaurant tipping and much more.

The discussions were audio-taped and I made verbatim transcripts of the tapes myself. Though time-consuming, this brought people to life again in my mind and caused me to pay close attention to every word, every inflection. The quotations from this interview material are set in bold in the text. When it came to analysing these transcripts I looked at the computer programs that are available for such purposes but chose not to use them for this project: there can be a tendency to over-process the data so that it ends up looking a bit like a quantitative exercise. Thus it remained very much a hands-on project, relying on my experience in qualitative research. For those who are interested in further reading about the rationales behind the method used — about focus groups and about analysis of qualitative material — the thesis contains all of this and is available through the University of Melbourne library system.[4]

Notes

Introduction

1 A.H. Quiggin, *A Survey of Primitive Money*, Methuen, London, 1949, p. 1.

2 V.A.StC. Wilson, 'Money: A Personal and Private Currency', PhD thesis, University of Melbourne, 1996.

3 The appendix at page 191 sets out more details about the research sample and the research methodology.

4 J. Buchan, *Frozen Desire: An Inquiry into the Meaning of Money*, Picador, UK, 1997.

Chapter 1—Money Has a Childhood

1 S. Maital, *Minds, Markets and Money: Psychological Foundations of Economic Behavior*, Basic Books, New York, 1982, p. 49.

2 C. Rubenstein, 'Money and self esteem, relationships, secrecy, envy, satisfaction', *Psychology Today*, May 1981.

3 See R.E. Lane, 'Money and the Varieties of Happiness', paper presented to the Annual Meeting of the International Society of Political Psychology, Oxford, 1983. Also see R.E. Lane, *The Market Experience*, Cambridge University Press, Cambridge, 1991. Also S. Maital, op. cit., 1982. And S.E.G. Lea, R.M. Tarpy and

P. Webley, *The Individual in the Economy*, Cambridge University Press, Cambridge, 1987.

4 S. Singh, *Marriage Money*, Allen & Unwin, Sydney, 1997, p. 49.; C. Rubenstein, op. cit., 1981.

5 S.E.G. Lea, P. Webley and R.M. Levine, 'The economic psychology of consumer debt', *Journal of Economic Psychology*, 14, 1993, pp. 85–119; A. Furnham and P. Thomas, 'Pocket money: a study of economic education', *British Journal of Developmental Psychology*, 2, 1984, pp. 205–11.

6 J. Pahl, *Money and Marriage*, Macmillan, London, 1989.

7 J.K. Galbraith, *Money: Whence It Came, Where It Went*, Penguin, London, 1975, p. 14.

8 A. Furnham, 'Why do people save? Attitudes to, and habits of, saving money in Britain', *Journal of Applied Social Psychology*, 15, 4, 1985, pp. 354–73.

9 G. Little, 'The uses of childhood', paper written for the International Society of Political Psychology, San Francisco, 1992.

Chapter 2—Touchstones: Money Coming Out

1 J.M. Keynes, *The Economic Consequences of the Peace*, Macmillan, London, 1919, p. 17.

2 E. Bergler, *Money and Emotional Conflicts*, International Universities Press, New York, 1951, p. 19.

3 N.T. Feather, 'Variables relating to the allocation of pocket money to children: parental reasons and values', *British Journal of Social Psychology*, 30, 1991, pp. 221–34.

4 H. Marshall and L. Magruder, 'Relations between parent money education practices and children's knowledge and use of money', *Child Development*, 31, 1960, pp. 253–84.

5 A. Furnham and P. Thomas, 'Pocket money: a study of economic education', *British Journal of Developmental Psychology*, 2, 1984, pp. 205–11.

6 V.A. Zelizer, *Pricing the Priceless Child*, Basic Books, New York, 1985, pp. 97 and 213. Also see V.A. Zelizer, 'The social meaning of money:"special monies"', *American Journal of Sociology*, 95, 1989, p. 368. Also see S. Singh, *Marriage Money*, Allen & Unwin, Sydney, 1997.

7 V.A. Zelizer, *The Social Meaning of Money*, Basic Books, New York, 1994, p. 66.

8 T. Wiseman, *The Money Motive*, Random House, New York, 1974, p. 14.

9 S. Klebanow and E.L. Lowenkopf (eds), *Money and Mind*, Plenum Press, New York, 1991, p. 54.

10 M. Edwards, *Financial Arrangements Within Families*, National Women's Advisory Council, Canberra, 1981.

11 C. Rubenstein, 'Money and self esteem, relationships, secrecy, envy, satisfaction', *Psychology Today*, May 1981, pp. 29–44.

Chapter 3—Expert-talk: Money in Economics

1 W.C. Neale, *Monies in Societies*, Chandler & Sharp Publishers, San Francisco, 1976, p. 7.

2 Neale points out (p. 16) that paper money existed in China centuries ago. Marco Polo reported the Chinese Emperor paying in a paper currency made from the inner bark of the mulberry tree, and insisting that it be accepted throughout his empire!

3 See C.P. Kindleberger, *A Financial History of Western Europe*, George Allen & Unwin, London, 1984, p. 85.

4 C. Menger, *Principles of Economics* [1871], trans. J. Dingwell and B.F. Hoselitz, New York University Press, New York, 1976 edn, p. 271.

5 See P.H. Kelly (ed.), *Locke on Money*, Clarendon Press, Oxford, 1991, p. 87.

6 T. Hobbes, *Leviathan* [1651], Everyman edn, London, 1943, p. 133.

7 A. Marshall, 'Mechanical and Biological Analogies in Economics' [1898], in A.C. Pigou (ed.), *Memorials of Alfred Marshall*, Kelley & Millman Inc., New York, 1956, p. 318.

8 K. Marx, *Capital*, 1 [1867], Vintage Books, New York, 1977 edn. Also K. Marx, *Early Writings*, trans. R. Livingstone and G. Benton, Penguin, London, 1975.

9 S. Maital, *Minds, Markets and Money*, Basic Books, New York, 1982, p. 15.

10 See J. Creedy and D.P. O'Brien (eds), *Economic Analysis in Historical Perspective*, Butterworths, UK, 1984. Also see New Palgrave Dictionary, 1992, pp. 770–4.

11 J.A. Schumpeter, *History of Economic Analysis*, Oxford University Press, London, 1954, p. 288.

12 R.E. Lane, *The Market Experience*, Cambridge University Press, Cambridge, 1991.

13 A. Smith, *An Inquiry into the Nature and Causes of the Wealth of Nations* [1776], repr. University of Chicago Press, Chicago, 1976.
14 H. Mackay, *Reinventing Australia*, Angus & Robertson, Sydney, 1993, p. 113.
15 H.M.J.J. Snelders, G. Hussein, S.E.G. Lea and P. Webley, 'The polymorphous concept of money', *Journal of Economic Psychology*, 13, 1992, pp. 71–92.

Chapter 4—What Can the Social Sciences Tell Us About Money?

1 K.T. Yamauchi and D.I. Templer, 'The development of a money attitude scale', *Journal of Personality Assessment*, 46, 5, 1982, p. 522.
2 A. Furnham, 'Many sides of the coin: the psychology of money usage', *Personality and Individual Difference*, 5, 5, 1984, p. 501.
3 R.E. Lane, *The Market Experience*, Cambridge University Press, Cambridge, 1991, pp. 59 and 99.
4 For detailed discussion of a range of psychological and economic research pertaining to money see S.E.G. Lea, R.M. Tarpy and P. Webley, *The Individual in the Economy*, Cambridge University Press, Cambridge, 1987; S. Maital, *Minds, Markets and Money*, Basic Books, New York, 1982; and R.E. Lane, *The Market Experience*, op. cit., 1991.
5 P.F. Wernimont and S. Fitzpatrick, 'The meaning of money', *Journal of Applied Psychology*, 56, 3, 1972, pp. 218–26.
6 C. Rubenstein, 'Money and self esteem, relationships, secrecy, envy, satisfaction', *Psychology Today*, May 1981, pp. 29–44.
7 A. Furnham, 'Many sides of the coin: the psychology of money usage', *Personality and Individual Difference*, 5, 5, 1984, pp. 501–9. There are several other important contributions to our understanding of money attitudes from Adrian Furnham. See Bibliography for details.
8 K.T. Yamauchi and D.I. Templer, op. cit., pp. 522–8.
9 T. Li-Ping Tang, 'The meaning of money revisited', *Journal of Organizational Behavior*, 13, 1992, pp. 197–202. Also 'The meaning of money: extension and exploration of the money ethic scale in a sample of university students in Taiwan', *Journal of Organizational Behavior*, 14, 1993, pp. 93–9.
10 V.A. Zelizer, *The Social Meaning of Money*, Basic Books, New York, 1994. Also *Pricing the Priceless Child*, Basic Books, New York, 1985.
11 V.A. Zelizer, 'The social meaning of money: "special monies"', *American Journal of Sociology*, 95, 1989, p. 352.

12 R.W. Belk and M. Wallendorf, 'The sacred meanings of money', *Journal of Economic Psychology*, 11, 1990, pp. 35–67.

13 M. Douglas, *Purity and Danger*, Routledge & Kegan Paul, London, 1966, p. 69.

14 See P. Webley, S.E.G. Lea and R. Portalska, 'The unacceptability of money as a gift', *Journal of Economic Psychology*, 4, 1983, pp. 223–8; G. Hussein, 'Is money an acceptable gift in Cyprus?' *Perceptual and Motor Skills*, 61, 1985; D. Cheal, *The Gift Economy*, Routledge, London, 1988; S. Cameron, 'The unacceptability of money as a gift and its status as a medium of exchange', *Journal of Economic Psychology*, 10, 1989, pp. 253–5; P. Webley and R. Wilson, 'Social relationships and the unacceptability of money as a gift', *Journal of Social Psychology*, 129, 1989, pp. 85–91; and C. Burgoyne and D.A. Routh, 'Constraints on the use of money as a gift at Christmas: the role of status and intimacy', *Journal of Economic Psychology*, 12, 1991, pp. 47–69.

15 C. Burgoyne and D.A. Routh, op. cit., 1991.

Chapter 5—Money, Freud and Control

1 S. Klebanow and E.L. Lowenkopf (eds), *Money and Mind*, Plenum Press, New York, 1991, p. 52.

2 S. Freud, *Collected Papers*, vols II and III [1924], The Hogarth Press and The Institute of Psycho-Analysis, London, 1956 edn.

3 O. Fenichel, 'The Drive to Amass Wealth' [1938], in *The Collected Papers of Otto Fenichel*, H. Fenichel and D. Rapaport (eds), Routledge & Kegan Paul, London, 1955, p. 98.

4 S. Freud, op. cit., 1956 edn, p. 50.

5 See E. Borneman (ed.), *The Psychoanalysis of Money*, Urizen Books, New York, 1976, p. 6.

6 E. Bergler, *Money and Emotional Conflicts*, International Universities Press, New York, 1951.

7 A. Furnham, 'Why do people save? Attitudes to, and habits of, saving money in Britain', *Journal of Applied Social Psychology*, 15, 4, 1985, pp. 354–73; A. Furnham and P. Thomas, 'Pocket money: a study of economic education', *British Journal of Developmental Psychology*, 2, 1984, pp. 205–11.

8 E. Jones, 'Anal-Erotic Character Traits' [1912], in *Papers on Psycho-Analysis*, Bailliere, Tindall and Cox, London, 1950 edn, p. 413.

9 C. Rubenstein, 'Money and self esteem, relationships, secrecy, envy, satisfaction', *Psychology Today*, May 1981.

10 E. Jones, op. cit., p. 419.
11 S.E.G. Lea, R.M. Tarpy and P. Webley, *The Individual in the Economy*, Cambridge University Press, Cambridge, 1987, pp. 237–8.
12 S. Freud, 'The Interpretation of Dreams' [1900], and 'Formulations on the Two Principles of Mental Functioning' [1925], in The Standard Edition of *The Complete Psychological Works of Sigmund Freud*, trans. J. Strachey, vols 5 and 12, The Hogarth Press and The Institute of Psycho-Analysis, London, 1953.
13 E.H. Erikson, *Childhood and Society* [1950], Penguin, London, 1965, pp. 239–66.
14 E.H. Erikson, op. cit., 1950.

Chapter 6—Controlling Yourself and Your Money

1 J. Pahl, *Money and Marriage*, Macmillan, London, 1989, pp. 128–31.
2 H. Mackay, *The Mackay Report: Money*, Mackay Research, New South Wales, 1984, p. 30.
3 S. Singh, *Marriage Money*, Allen & Unwin, Sydney, 1997, pp. 126–35.
4 R.E. Lane, *The Market Experience*, Cambridge University Press, Cambridge, 1991, p. 104.
5 See *The Mackay Report: Money*, op. cit., 1984 and H. Mackay, *Marketscan: The Banking Market*, 1992. Also S. Singh, op. cit., 1997.
6 S.E.G. Lea, R.M. Tarpy and P. Webley, *The Individual in the Economy*, Cambridge University Press, Cambridge, 1987, pp. 216 and 227–8.
7 E. Bergler, *Money and Emotional Conflicts*, International Universities Press, New York, 1951; J.M. Keynes, *The General Theory of Employment, Interest and Money* [1936], Macmillan, London, 1973 edn, p. 108; Jane Austen, *Mansfield Park* [1814], Penguin Classics, London, 1985.
8 T. Veblen, The Theory of the Leisure Class [1899], in *The Writings of Thorstein Veblen*, Reprints of Economic Classics, Augustus M. Kelley, New York, 1975.
9 R.E. Lane, op. cit., 1991, p. 106.
10 P.F. Wernimont and S. Fitzpatrick, 'The meaning of money', *Journal of Applied Psychology*, 56, 3, 1972, pp. 218–26.
11 A. Furnham, 'Why do people save? Attitudes to, and habits of, saving money in Britain', *Journal of Applied Social Psychology*, 15, 4, 1985, pp. 354–73.

Chapter 7—Of Milk and Money

1 M. Klein, *Envy and Gratitude*, Tavistock Publications, London, 1957.
2 T. Wiseman, *The Money Motive*, Random House, New York, 1974, p. 49.
3 E.V. Wolfenstein, in *Political Psychology*, vol. 14, no. 2, June 1993, p. 307.
4 E. Bergler, *Money and Emotional Conflicts*, International Universities Press, New York, 1951, p. 135.
5 S. Freud, *Collected Papers*, vols II and III [1924], The Hogarth Press and The Institute of Psycho-Analysis, London, 1956, p. 351.
6 *Sunday Age*, 15/9/96.
7 D.W. Krueger (ed.), *The Last Taboo: Money as Symbol and Reality in Psychotherapy and Psychoanalysis*, Brunner/Mazel Publishers, New York, 1986. See also S. Klebanow and E.L. Lowenkopf (eds), *Money and Mind*, Plenum Press, New York, 1991.
8 The *Age*, 4/5/96.
9 G. Simmel, *The Philosophy of Money* [1907], D. Frisby (ed.), trans. T. Bottomley and D. Frisby, Routledge, London, 1990, p. 376.
10 A. Roy, *The God of Small Things*, Flamingo, London, 1997.
11 H. Garner, *The First Stone*, Pan Macmillan, Australia, 1995, p. 173; G. Simmel, op. cit., pp. 219–20.
12 D. Lodge, *Therapy*, Secker & Warburg, London, 1995, p. 67.
13 R.W. Belk and M. Wallendorf, 'The sacred meanings of money', *Journal of Economic Psychology*, 11, 1990, p. 53.
14. J. Pahl, *Money and Marriage*, Macmillan, London, 1989, p. 76.
15 E.M. Hallowell and W.J. Grace, 'Money styles', in *Money and Mind*, S. Klebanow and E.L. Lowenkopf (eds), op. cit., 1991, p. 15.
16 A.F. Davies, *Skills, Outlooks and Passions: A Psychoanalytic Contribution to the Study of Politics*, Cambridge University Press, Cambridge, 1980, pp. 346–60.
17 T. Veblen, 'The Theory of the Leisure Class' [1899], in *The Writings of Thorstein Veblen*, Reprints of Economic Classics, Augustus M. Kelley, New York, 1975, p. 110.
18 N.W. Aldrich, *Old Money*, Vintage Books, New York, 1988.
19 L. Lapham, *Money and Class in America*, Weidenfeld & Nicolson, New York, 1988.

Chapter 8—Control Becomes Power

1 M. Edwards, *Financial Arrangements within Families*, National Women's Advisory Council, Canberra, 1981; J. Pahl, *Money and Marriage*, Macmillan, London, 1989; C. Vogler and J. Pahl, 'Money, power and inequality within marriage', *Sociological Review*, 42, 2, 1994, pp. 263–88.

2 See, for example, B. Berger, 'The Social Roots of Prosperity', 1995 John Bonython Lecture, *CIS Occasional Papers* 55, The Centre for Independent Studies, Sydney, 1996, p. 8.

3 S. Singh, *Marriage Money*, Allen & Unwin, Sydney, 1997.

4 O. Fenichel, 'The Drive to Amass Wealth' [1938], in *The Collected Papers of Otto Fenichel*, H. Fenichel and D. Rapaport (eds), Routledge & Kegan Paul, London, 1955, pp. 90–102.

5 It is important to remember a sample 'bias' here: the female focus-group discussions were held during the day and consisted of women who were primarily home-based carers at the time, though most had some part-time employment.

6 N. Wolf, *Fire With Fire*, Vintage Books, UK, 1994.

7 S. Singh, op. cit., 1997.

8 See, for example, S.E.G. Lea, P. Webley and R.M. Levine, 'The economic psychology of consumer debt', *Journal of Economic Psychology*, 14, 1993, pp. 85–119.

9 H. Mackay, *The Mackay Report: Money*, and *Marketscan: The Banking Market*, Mackay Research, New South Wales, 1984 and 1992.

10 M. Lynn and B. Latane, 'The psychology of restaurant tipping', *Journal of Applied Social Psychology*, 14, 6, 1984, pp. 549–61; A.H. Crusco and C.G. Wetzel, 'The Midas touch: the effects of interpersonal touch on restaurant tipping', *Personality and Social Psychology Bulletin*, 10, 4, 1984, pp. 512–17.

11 S. Freeman, M.R. Walker, R. Borden and B. Latane, 'Diffusion of responsibility and restaurant tipping: cheaper by the bunch', *Personality and Social Psychology Bulletin*, 1, 4, 1975, pp. 584–7; M.L. Snyder, 'The inverse relationship between restaurant party size and tip percentage: diffusion of responsibility or equity?', *Personality and Social Psychology Bulletin*, Sum. 2, 3, 1976, p. 308.

12 M. Lynn and B. Latane, op. cit., 1984.

13 C. McGregor, *Profile of Australia*, Penguin, Melbourne, 1968, p. 50.

14 V.A. Zelizer, *The Social Meaning of Money*, Basic Books, New York, 1994, pp. 95–6.

15 D. Cheal, *The Gift Economy*, Routledge, London, 1988, pp. 1–9.
16 M. Millman, *Warm Hearts and Cold Cash: The Intimate Dynamics of Families and Money*, The Free Press, New York, 1991, p. 56.
17 Juvenal, c. A.D. 60–140.
18 R.W. Belk and M. Wallendorf, 'The sacred meanings of money', *Journal of Economic Psychology*, 11, 1990, pp. 35–67; V.A. Zelizer, 'The social meaning of money: "special monies"', *American Journal of Sociology*, 95, 1989, pp. 342–77.
19 T. Wiseman, *The Money Motive*, Random House, New York, 1974, pp. 251–2.
20 M. Millman, op. cit., 1991, pp. 2–3.
21 D.W. Tresemer, *Fear of Success*, Plenum Press, New York, 1977, pp. 22–3.
22 C. Rubenstein, 'Money and self esteem, relationships, secrecy, envy, satisfaction', *Psychology Today*, May 1981, p. 39.

Chapter 9—Money, Gender and Sex

1 *Robin Hood Was Right: A Guide to Giving Your Money for Social Change*, Vanguard Public Foundation, California, 1977.
2 S. Klebanow and E.L. Lowenkopf (eds), *Money and Mind*, Plenum Press, New York, 1991, pp. 57–8.
3 Jacques Lacan (1903–1981) was a French psychoanalytic practitioner and theorist. I am grateful to Dr Graham Little for pointing out this aspect of Lacan's thinking. See John Forrester's essays *Truth Games: Lies, Money, and Psychoanalysis*, Harvard University Press, Cambridge, Mass., 1997.
4 See M. Prince, 'Self-concept, money beliefs and values' and 'Women, men and money styles', both in *Journal of Economic Psychology*, 14, 1993, pp. 161–73 and 175–82; also J. Pahl, *Money and Marriage*, Macmillan, London, 1989.
5 C. Gilligan, *In a Different Voice*, Harvard University Press, Cambridge, Mass., 1982.
6 M. Millman, *Warm Hearts and Cold Cash*, The Free Press, New York, 1991, pp. 82–4.
7 See, for example, D.W. Tresemer, *Fear of Success*, Plenum Press, New York, 1977; C. Rubenstein, 'Money and self esteem, relationships, secrecy, envy, satisfaction', *Psychology Today*, May 1981; J. Pahl, *Money and Marriage*, Macmillan, London, 1989; S. Klebanow, 'Power, gender and money', in *Money and Mind*; S. Klebanow and E.L. Lowenkopf (eds), Plenum Press, New York, 1991.

8 N. Wolf, *Fire With Fire*, Vintage Books, UK, 1994, p. 261.
9 T. Wiseman, *The Money Motive*, Random House, New York, 1974, pp. 212–14.
10 S. Singh, 'Marriage, Money and Information: Australian Consumers' Use of Banks', PhD thesis, LaTrobe University, Victoria, 1994, p. 199.
11 C.B. Burgoyne and D.A. Routh, 'Constraints on the use of money as a gift at Christmas: the role of status and intimacy', *Journal of Economic Psychology*, 12, 1991, pp. 47–69.
12 R.M. Titmuss, *The Gift Relationship*, George Allen & Unwin, London, 1970.

Chapter 10—Balancing the Books: Personal and Impersonal Currency

1 D.W. Krueger (ed.), *The Last Taboo: Money as Symbol and Reality in Psychotherapy and Psychoanalysis*, Brunner/Mazel Publishers, New York, 1986, p. 3.
2 See Roy Morgan Research Financial Monitors.
3 See S. Maital, *Minds, Markets and Money*, Basic Books, New York, 1982, pp. 219ff.
4 Source: ANZ Bank Savings Reports. See also 'Measuring Australia's Economy', edn 4, cat. no. 1360.0, 1996, pp. 98–9, Australian Bureau of Statistics, Canberra, which confirms this downward trend in household savings.
5 OECD Economic Outlook, June 1998, Annex Table 26.
6 S. Maital, op. cit., 1982, pp. 134–46.
7 The *Age*, 24/9/95.

Chapter 11—The Secret Life of Money

1 D.W. Krueger (ed.), *The Last Taboo: Money as Symbol and Reality in Psychotherapy and Psychoanalysis*, Brunner/Mazel Publishers, New York, 1986, p. vii.
2 R.W. Belk and M. Wallendorf, 'The sacred meanings of money', *Journal of Economic Psychology*, 11, 1990, p. 61.
3 T. Wiseman, *The Money Motive*, Random House, New York, 1974, p. 107.
4 J. Pahl, *Money and Marriage*, Macmillan, London, 1989, p. 126.
5 D.W. Krueger (ed.), op. cit., 1986, p. ix.
6 S. Klebanow and E.L. Lowenkopf (eds), *Money and Mind*, Plenum Press, New York, 1991, pp. vii–viii.

7 E.H. Erikson, *Childhood and Society* [1950], Penguin, London, 1965, pp. 243–6.

8 P.F. Wernimont and S. Fitzpatrick, 'The meaning of money', *Journal of Applied Psychology*, 56, 3, 1972, p. 220.

9 B. Blouin (ed.), *The Legacy of Inherited Wealth*, Trio Press, Canada, 1995.

10 M. Shell, *Money, Language, and Thought*, University of California Press, Calif., 1982, p. 180.

11 D.N. McCloskey, *The Rhetoric of Economics*, The University of Wisconsin Press, Wisconsin, 1985, p. xvii.

12 The *Age*, 18/9/96.

13 In S. Klebanow and E.L. Lowenkopf (eds), *Money and Mind*, Plenum Press, New York, 1991, pp. 15–16.

14 The *Age*, 1/12/96.

15 See *London Review of Books*, September 1997.

Appendix—The Research Method and Sample

1 D.N. McCloskey, *The Rhetoric of Economics*, The University of Wisconsin Press, Wisconsin, 1985.

2 It is difficult to measure precisely the proportion of the population of Anglo-Celtic background. In *Dimensions of Australian Society* (1994), Graetz and McAllister suggest that in 1978 people 'of British origin' comprised 76.9 per cent (a fall from 90 per cent in 1947). Their projection for 2008 is that this sector will still represent 70.6 per cent of the Australian population. Singh's 1994 study of Anglo-Celts and banking put the proportion at around 50 per cent (doctoral thesis, LaTrobe University). Whatever the precise figure, or the precise method of calculating 'background' — which is more complicated than birthplace, or even parents' birthplace — Australians of Anglo-Celtic background still represent a significant sector of the overall population: at least half, and possibly almost three-quarters.

3 See C.E. Osgood and J.C Snider (eds), *Semantic Differential Technique: A Sourcebook*, Aldine, Chicago, 1969. C.E. Osgood, G.J. Suci and P.H. Tannenbaum, *The Measurement of Meaning*, University of Illinois Press, Urbana, 1957.

4 V.A.St.C. Wilson, 'Money: A Personal and Private Currency', PhD thesis, University of Melbourne, 1996.

Selected Bibliography

In a cross-disciplinary project, the background reading necessarily covers a wide field. This was even more so for a subject such as money which can be approached from so many different angles. All texts that have been quoted in the book are listed in the endnotes for the relevant chapter and do not necessarily appear again in this bibliographical list. The following is an abbreviated list of some of the main texts that readers may find of interest. Those marked with an asterisk survey the major research across both psychology and economics and are particularly useful.

Aldrich, N.W., *Old Money*, Vintage Books, New York, 1988.

Belk, R.W. and Wallendorf, M., 'The sacred meanings of money', *Journal of Economic Psychology*, 11, 1990, pp. 35–67.

Bergler, E., *Money and Emotional Conflicts*, International Universities Press, New York, 1951.

Borneman, E. (ed.), *The Psychoanalysis of Money* [1973], trans. M. Shaw, Urizen Books, New York, 1976.

Cheal, D., *The Gift Economy*, Routledge, London, 1988.

Creedy, J. and O'Brien, D.P. (eds), *Economic Analysis in Historical Perspective*, Butterworths, United Kingdom, 1984.

Crump, T., *The Phenomenon of Money*, Routledge & Kegan Paul, London, 1981.

Erikson, E.H., *Childhood and Society* [1950], Penguin, London, 1965.
Fenichel, O., 'The Drive to Amass Wealth' [1938], in *The Collected Papers of Otto Fenichel*, H. Fenichel and D. Rapaport (eds), Routledge & Kegan Paul, London, 1955.
Ferenczi, S., 'The Ontogenesis of the Interest in Money' [1916], in *First Contributions to Psycho-Analysis*, trans. E. Jones, The Hogarth Press and The Institute of Psycho-Analysis, London, 1952.
Freud, S., 'The Interpretation of Dreams' [1900], in *The Standard Edition of The Complete Psychological Works of Sigmund Freud*, trans. J. Strachey, vol. 5, The Hogarth Press and The Institute of Psycho-Analysis, London, 1953.
—— *Collected Papers* [1908], trans. J. Riviere, Basic Books, New York, 1959.
—— *Collected Papers*, vols II and III [1924], The Hogarth Press and The Institute of Psycho-Analysis, London 1956 edn.
—— 'Formulations on the Two Principles of Mental Functioning' [1925], in *The Standard Edition of The Complete Psychological Works of Sigmund Freud*, vol. 12, trans. J. Strachey, The Hogarth Press and The Institute of Psycho-Analysis, London, 1953.
Furnham, A. 'Many sides of the coin: the psychology of money usage', *Personality and Individual Difference*, 5, 5, 1984, pp. 501–9.
—— 'Why do people save? Attitudes to, and habits of, saving money in Britain', *Journal of Applied Social Psychology*, 15, 4, 1985, pp. 354–73.
—— 'The structure of economic beliefs', *Personality and Individual Difference*, 8, 2, 1987, pp. 253–60.
Furnham, A. and Thomas, P., 'Pocket money: a study of economic education', *British Journal of Developmental Psychology*, 2, 1984, pp. 205–11.
Furnham, A. and Rose, M., 'Alternative ethics: the relationship between the wealth, welfare, work and leisure ethic', *Human Relations*, 40, 9, 1987, pp. 561–74.
Furth, H.G., *The World of Grown-Ups: Children's Conceptions of Society*, Elsevier, New York, 1980.
Galbraith, J.K., *The Affluent Society*, Penguin Edition, London, 1958.
—— *Money: Whence It Came, Where It Went*, Penguin Edition, London, 1975.
—— *The Culture of Contentment*, Houghton Mifflin Co., New York, 1992.
Gellerman, S.W, *Motivation and Productivity*, American Management Association Inc., New York, 1963.

Gilligan, C., *In a Different Voice*, Harvard University Press, Cambridge, Mass., 1982.

*Goldberg, H. and Lewis, R.T., *Money Madness: The Psychology of Saving, Spending, Loving and Hating Money*, Signet Books, New York, 1978.

Graetz, B. and McAllister, I., *Dimensions of Australian Society* (2nd edn), Macmillan, Melbourne, 1994.

Hobbes, T., *Leviathan* [1651], Everyman edn, London, 1943.

Jones, E., 'Anal-Erotic Character Traits' [1912], in *Papers on Psycho-Analysis*, (5th edn), Bailliere, Tindall & Cox, London, 1950.

Kelly, P.H. (ed.), *Locke on Money*, Clarendon Press, Oxford, 1991.

Keynes, J.M., *The Economic Consequences of the Peace*, Macmillan, London, 1919.

—— *A Treatise on Money*, vol.1, Macmillan, London, 1930.

—— *The General Theory of Employment, Interest and Money* [1936], Macmillan, London, 1973 edn.

Kindleberger, C.P., *A Financial History of Western Europe*, George Allen & Unwin, London, 1984.

Klebanow, S. and Lowenkopf, E.L. (eds), *Money and Mind*, Plenum Press, New York, 1991.

Klein, M., *Envy and Gratitude*, Tavistock Publications, London, 1957.

Krueger, D.W. (ed.), *The Last Taboo: Money as Symbol and Reality in Psychotherapy and Psychoanalysis*, Brunner/Mazel Publishers, New York, 1986.

*Lane, R.E., *The Market Experience*, Cambridge University Press, Cambridge, 1991.

*Lea, S.E.G., Tarpy, R.M. and Webley, P., *The Individual in the Economy*, Cambridge University Press, Cambridge, 1987.

Levine, D.N., *The Flight From Ambiguity*, University of Chicago Press, Chicago, 1985.

Mackay, H., *Reinventing Australia*, Angus & Robertson, Sydney, 1993.

*Maital, S., *Minds, Markets and Money*, Basic Books, New York, 1982.

Marshall, A., 'Mechanical and Biological Analogies in Economics' [1898], in *Memorials of Alfred Marshall*, A.C. Pigou (ed.), Kelley & Millman Inc., New York, 1956.

Marshall, H. and Magruder, L., 'Relations between parent money education practices and children's knowledge and use of money', *Child Development*, 31, 1960, pp. 253–84.

Marx, K., *Early Writings* [1859], trans. R. Livingstone and G. Benton, Penguin, London, 1975.

—— *Capital, 1* [1867], Vintage Books, New York, 1977 edn.

McCloskey D.N., *The Rhetoric of Economics*, The University of Wisconsin Press, Wisconsin, 1985.

Menger, C., *Principles of Economics* [1871], trans. J. Dingwall and B.F. Hoselitz, New York University Press, New York, 1976 edn.

Mill, J.S., 'On the influence of consumption upon production' [1829], in *Essays on Some Unsettled Questions of Political Economy*, London School of Economics and Political Science, Aldwych, London, 1948.

Millman, M., *Warm Hearts and Cold Cash*, The Free Press, New York, 1991.

*Neale, W.C., *Monies in Societies*, Chandler & Sharp Publishers, San Francisco, 1976.

Pahl, J., *Money and Marriage*, Macmillan, London, 1989.

Parry, J. and Bloch, M. (eds), *Money and the Morality of Exchange*, Cambridge University Press, Cambridge, 1989.

Quiggin, A.H., *A Survey of Primitive Money*, Methuen, London, 1949.

Rubenstein, C., 'Money and self esteem, relationships, secrecy, envy, satisfaction', *Psychology Today*, May 1981, pp. 29–44.

Schumpeter, J.A., *History of Economic Analysis*, Oxford University Press, Oxford, 1954.

Shell, M., *Money, Language, and Thought*, University of California Press, California, 1982.

Simmel, G., *The Philosophy of Money* [1907], D. Frisby (ed.), trans. T. Bottomley and D. Frisby, Routledge, London, 1990.

Singh, S., *Marriage Money*, Allen & Unwin, Sydney, 1997.

Smith, A., *An Inquiry into the Nature and Causes of the Wealth of Nations* [1776], repr. University of Chicago Press, Chicago, 1976.

Tawney, R.H., *Religion and the Rise of Capitalism* [1926], Pelican, United Kingdom, 1938.

Titmuss, R.M., *The Gift Relationship*, George Allen & Unwin, London, 1970.

Veblen, T., 'The Theory of the Leisure Class' [1899], in *The Writings of Thorstein Veblen*, Reprints of Economic Classics, Augustus M. Kelley, New York, 1975.

Weber, M., *The Protestant Ethic and the Spirit of Capitalism*, Scribner, New York, 1958.

Winnicott, D.W., *Playing and Reality* [1971], Penguin, London, 1974.

*Wiseman, T., *The Money Motive*, Random House, New York, 1974.

Zelizer, V.A., *Pricing the Priceless Child*, Basic Books, New York, 1985.

—— *The Social Meaning of Money*, Basic Books, New York, 1994.

Index